Living
Kabbalah

© 2008, 2010 Kabbalah Centre International, Inc.

Kabbalah Publishing is a registered DBA of
Kabbalah Centre International, Inc.

For further information:

The Kabbalah Centre
155 E. 48th St., New York, NY 10017
1062 S. Robertson Blvd., Los Angeles, CA 90035

1.800.Kabbalah
www.kabbalah.com

First Edition, January 2008
First Trade Paperback Edition, July 2010
Printed in USA

ISBN13: 978-1-57189-660-5

Design: HL Design (Hyun Min Lee) www.hldesignco.com

Yehuda Berg

Living

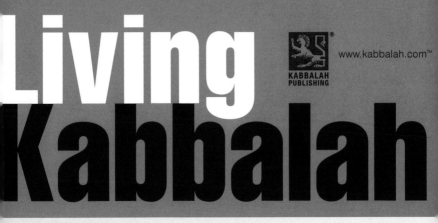

KABBALAH
PUBLISHING

www.kabbalah.com™

Kabbalah

A Practical System
for Making the Power
Work for You

This book is dedicated to the talented Living Kabbalah team who helped to make The Living Kabbalah audio System possible. To Shore Slocum, Jill Blessing, and Rachel Kowalski, the process we shared in putting the wisdom of Kabbalah into an audio format inspired me to my next level. Thank you.

Table of Contents

VI. Corrections & Consciousness

VIII. Vessel

XI. Sharing

Introduction

We are about to embark on a journey together—a journey that will be very personal, meaningful and, at times, a little uncomfortable. Over the next twenty-three chapters, we will embrace some amazing opportunities for growth, which will lead us to the clarity of purpose we have been seeking.

Maybe we've been wandering off-course for a while, assailed by our fears, undermined by a sense of emptiness in our lives, drained by our compulsive and addictive behaviors. How did we get so far off track? More importantly, how do we get ourselves back on course and remain there? The wisdom of Kabbalah will help us answer these important questions. Kabbalah is about action; it's not some cryptic philosophy. With this in mind, we ask that you be practical. We ask that you be open. We ask that you NOT believe everything that we will share with you in this book until you explore it, test it out, and see what it means for you personally.

Each chapter in this book builds upon the previous one, so it's important that you complete the exercises and meditation at the end of each section before you move on. Kabbalah tools—which we call k-Tools—will help reveal new insights that will lead to profound changes in your perspective, awareness, and actions, and each step builds on the one that came before.

From the time I was born, my life has been intimately connected to Kabbalah. As a child our home brimmed with students seeking to better understand this ancient wisdom. The Kabbalah that I have studied throughout my life is the Kabbalah that I will be sharing with you in this book, some of which has never been revealed before in the way you'll read it here.

Throughout my life I have had the greatest mentors a kabbalist could ask for. My father and teacher, Rav Berg, is one of the leading kabbalists in the world today. His teacher, Rav Ashlag, was the first person to translate Kabbalah into modern-day language, making it accessible to all who sought its wisdom. In fact, my father and my mother and teacher, Karen Berg, opened the pathway of Kabbalah to the world at large. A hundred years ago, very few people knew Kabbalah existed. Today, Kabbalah is greeted worldwide with recognition and respect.

What makes Kabbalah different?

There are four things that make Kabbalah different from anything else I've touched or studied.

1. Kabbalists believe in **constant change**. In order to get to the next level—to really transform—we must constantly change, day by day, hour by hour. It doesn't happen overnight. Kabbalah is not a pill that we take that instantly transforms our lives. Real transformation requires incremental change. When we finish level one, there's level two. After that, there's level three, and on and on the levels go. That's because there is a great deal we must transform in ourselves in order to reach our true potential. Out of necessity, it will take time and constant change to reach this ultimate fulfillment. The good news is that before long, you'll see changes in your life that will support your efforts.

2. The **tools** that Kabbalah offers—tools that may not make sense at the beginning—are tools that have been tested throughout the generations and found effective by millions of people. At this moment, we don't need to know exactly how or why they work so well. If you think about it, most of us don't even know how our phones work. How can we be in a boat near Singapore and talk to someone in a tent in Africa? We don't know exactly. But there is no question that when we dialed the number, the person on the other end picked up the phone. In much the same way, people use Kabbalah's spiritual tools—like the Red String, for example. We don't need to know the mechanics of how it works in order to know that the power of the Red String goes far beyond thread and dye.

3. The **lineage** of Kabbalah goes all the way back to Abraham in the Garden of Eden, when he received the book of Kabbalah from the angel Raziel. Moses received Kabbalah as an oral transmission on Mt. Sinai from the Creator, along with the physical Bible used today. I can trace my lineage to my teacher (my father), to the wisdom he received from his teacher, and the wisdom his teacher received from his master—all the way back to the Ari, Rav Isaac Luria, five hundred years ago. The Ari traces his own lineage back 2,000 more years to Rav Shimon bar Yochai, the author of the *Zohar*.

4. Kabbalah believes in the **big picture**. Our goal is to remove chaos and suffering from the entire world, not only from individuals. If our life is perfect but our family, our neighbor or community is experiencing chaos, we will also experience pain. Only when chaos has been abolished on the global scale will we be truly free to live joyfully.

Truth Resonates

Kabbalah is based on universal truths, and universal truths sound familiar to our hearts and minds. When we hear a universal truth, we feel as though we have heard the idea before; the words resonate in our Soul. We find ourselves saying: "Ah, that makes sense."

Our goal at the Kabbalah Centre—in teaching, studying, and being involved in this ancient wisdom—is to raise our own individual consciousness as well as that of other students who share our journey, and elevate the consciousness of the entire world. We do this so we can understand more about the Universe and its laws of cause and effect. We do this as a way of acknowledging that we're all in this boat together. If we damage our planetary vessel, we're not going to sink alone; the world is going to sink along with us. But together we can learn to stop drilling holes in the boat and hurting others. And that is just the beginning.

So let's begin the journey of a lifetime.

Lasting Fulfillment

Chapter 1

What You Desire

To make progress on any journey, first we have to identify where we are presently and what our destination is. Only then can we figure out the most efficient, effective route to get to where we want to go. So, let's take a moment to make these distinctions.

<u>List 1</u>: Write down everything you could possibly want in your life that could bring you fulfillment and a sense of security. Imagine it, having total peace of mind. Imagine how incredible that would feel! You could stop worrying, stop feeling lost, and stop feeling lonely. You'd have total clarity, great relationships, a sense of meaning and purpose, and a solid place in your community. List those things that would put you in that space.

<u>List 2</u>: Write down everything in your life that you don't want, like more panic attacks, depression, or partners who are emotionally unavailable. Maybe you'd like to stop smoking, or overeating, or drinking. Be specific and personal. This is about you. This will be your "before" picture.

A Bigger Vessel

Now ask yourself: "Is my life really all it could be right now?"

We can get more in our lives if we become more. I'm amazed sometimes by how small—how limited—our thinking can be. When someone asks us what we want out of the whole Universe, we find ourselves saying that we want one little thing, just this or that.

This reminds me of a story. A man wakes up in the morning and decides to go fishing. He goes to the docks, sits down, pulls out his fishing line, and and throws it in the water. On the dock, there's another fisherman who seems to be catching quite a few fish. With every fish this fisherman catches, he takes it to the side of the dock where there is a ruler. After measuring each fish, he keeps some and throws back others. After observing this behavior for some time, the man approaches the other fisherman and says: "What's up? Why are you throwing some fish back and keeping others? What are you looking for?"

The fisherman says, "I've got a twelve-inch pot in my house. The only ones I keep are the ones under twelve inches. Fish that are bigger, I can't use, so I throw them away."

Maybe it's time for a bigger pot!

Like the fisherman, we limit ourselves without even realizing it. We're trying to fit the Universe's infinite abundance into our small pot! The Universe wants to give us everything, but we're stuck with a tiny vessel that can't receive all that is available to us. What would happen if we expanded our vessel instead of placing limits on our abundance? It's time to upgrade our vessel in order to receive more by acknowledging what would truly give us fulfillment.

What do you really want from life?

I've asked that question of many people around the world, and it's amazing to me how universal the answers are. People want more money, a nice car, a comfortable house, and good health. They will say they want more fulfillment, happiness, and passion, but they're not always interested in doing the deeper work that is required to bring those things into their lives.

Let's try to better understand this whole notion of fulfillment, happiness, and passion. You can't intellectualize these things or even tap into them emotionally; you have to experience them. If you aren't experiencing it, you are limited by the inability to give it away to others, since you can only give what you have. If someone is a cynic or skeptical, can they encourage excitement and optimism in others? If someone is depressed, can they uplift you or give you a shot of passion?

We often attempt to create a sensation of excitement through some kind of external stimulus. A cigarette. Drugs. Alcohol. We overeat. All these substances give us a sense of temporary satisfaction. Then along comes Kabbalah with this simple message: you're never going to know true meaning and purpose over time if you keep trying to add up smaller and smaller experiences of short-lived excitement. That's not how it works. Kabbalah encourages us to expand who we are by sharing, in order to achieve a lasting flow of fulfillment—not the fleeting variety that lets us down again and again.

But Kabbalah is not just about achieving self-fulfillment. That's one of the aspects of Kabbalah that I love the most. Sometimes, the more we work on ourselves, the more self-absorbed we tend to become. Not with Kabbalah. With Kabbalah, it's not about *I-me-mine*; it's about our relationship with others and the world.

We live in trying times. We watch the news and hear about how someone just killed his family or how a child was abused or neglected. Global warming is generating record-breaking storms and extreme weather. Our water is in low supply, or contaminated. The world has gone crazy. At the same time, there is more spiritual Light and information being revealed than ever before. These two realities are occurring simultaneously: revelation and darkness. And that is one of the reasons why Kabbalah is rising in public awareness these days. Fifty years ago, no one even knew the word Kabbalah, let alone what it meant. Today, there are millions of people studying Kabbalah. We need this wisdom now more than ever because of the chaos that is thriving in the world today.

We turn to Kabbalah, because the antidote for chaos can be found there.

The Lineage of Kabbalah

The first real kabbalist was Abraham, who wrote *the Book of Formation*. He's known in the Bible as the father of religion, but he was also a kabbalist. Next came Moses, who not only brought down the physical Ten Commandments and spiritual knowledge in the form of the Bible, but also orally conveyed practical kabbalistic tools for living a good life.

The oral tradition was passed from teacher to student, again and again, until around 2,000 years ago, when Kabbalist Shimon bar Yochai authored the foundational text of Kabbalah, called the *Zohar*. He decreed that no one would study it for yet another thousand years, because the world wasn't ready for the language and technology it offered.

Around the 14th century, Kabbalah started to emerge from complete secrecy. There were Christian kabbalists in Italy and Spain. The actual *Zohar*, the sacred text of Kabbalah, where all this wisdom comes from, is said to have been dug up by the Knights Templar in Jerusalem and brought back to Europe. That's when the power of the *Zohar* began making itself known. Interestingly, it was at this time that the Grail legend first appeared. Some say that the Holy Grail is a book, possibly the *Zohar*, but there is no physical evidence of this. We can only speculate.

Since then, there have been some very famous people who were kabbalists. Isaac Newton, for example, had his own version of the *Zohar* in Latin, and he notes that Plato went to Egypt to study Kabbalah. Another great thinker that studied Kabbalah was

Pythagoras, who would climb Mount Carmel dressed in white like a high priest, and meditate.

The Power of Kabbalah

There are many myths and misconceptions about Kabbalah. Some of the most widespread are that one must be Jewish, male, and a rabbinical scholar over the age of 40 in order to study it. In the past that was true, because the information was so complex and because people were being killed simply for having this wisdom.

Why? Because any new technology can be seen as very threatening.

Imagine if you went back in time to the 1400s with your iPod or cellular phone and showed people this technology. They would think you were a witch or a wizard. The technology of Kabbalah is so advanced and powerful that, in essence, if you understand its wisdom, you don't need a priest, rabbi, or guru to do the work for you. You don't need anyone to stand as an intermediary between you and the Creator. All you need is you and the source of energy to which the wisdom of Kabbalah helps you connect. You don't need a middleman anymore, and that's very threatening to religious authorities. I was thrown out of school a few times because my father was a kabbalist. My parents have been physically beaten. My mom even ended up in a hospital with a concussion because of her involvement with Kabbalah.

But you know what? Nothing stopped this knowledge from coming out.

Although religion was given to humankind to unify us, to bring us together for a higher purpose, nothing has caused more separation and killing than organized religion. The righteousness and divisiveness of some people involved in religion has led to countless wars and mass bloodshed. On the other hand, Kabbalah encourages us to come together as one, to use our connection to the Creator—God, Allah, Jesus, Buddha, or whatever you want to call that God force—to unite under that energy.

One of the profound reasons I devote my life's work to helping people understand how to get out of their own way by using the wisdom of Kabbalah is because there is a purpose to it. It's not just a philosophy to be discussed over dinner. Kabbalah has the power to remove pain, suffering, and chaos in the world. Who would not want to be on board with that higher purpose? Who wouldn't want to be part of a Dream Team working toward that end?

So, what do you want from life?

One of my favorite spiritual Laws of the Universe, which we'll discuss later, is that *there is no coercion*. In other words, we can't force a desire upon someone else. Can I convince you what qualities you should want in a soul mate? No. You probably want different qualities in a soul mate than I do. We each have unique desires, and Universal Law recognizes this.

Similarly, Kabbalah says that in order to achieve happiness, you have to desire it first. Then you have to earn it. You have to go for it. We are here to create our own meaning, our own fulfillment. Kabbalah is about freedom; it's about being liberated and uninhibited. Kabbalah shows us the big picture and helps us to understand why we're here, and where we're going, which kindles our desire.

Many people are wandering around simply trying to get by, as if life is some kind of endurance test. That's exhausting! Life is meant to be exciting; there is a purpose to it. It's like a game and, like any game, there are rules. When we understand the rules of the game of life, we can win. We can also enjoy the process. In Kabbalah, we have a team of people who are right there with us and together we can create happiness that includes unity. To me, there is nothing more exciting than that.

Finding Your Way

When we understand the rules of the Game of Life, and empower people with these rules, it's like showing someone a map. If we've never been to a town before and we plan to drive into this town to find a particular location, what do we do? We get out a map or go online to get directions. Even if we're nervous about being in a foreign environment, we follow the directions and the map tells us what is going to appear next on our journey. Wow, there's that street! And here's this street! After a while, we gain confidence in the map. And by the time we've been driving for a while, we stop questioning it. We begin to trust the intentions and competence of the map maker. We understand that the map is there to help us.

Do we have to follow the map? Do we have to consult it? Do we have to go down every single road the map illustrates? No. We can choose to go in any direction we want. We can either take advantage of the wisdom, or we can ignore it completely. That's the beauty of free will.

What I've always appreciated about Kabbalah, and what I think other students with whom I have spoken also love about it, is that we can choose which path we want. Ultimately, whether we're Catholic or Hindu, black or white, European or American, we all can benefit from this wisdom. It's a bit like computer technology. We have five-year-olds today who know how to draw a graphic on a computer and print it out themselves. It's unbelievable. Imagine if that information had stayed limited only to computer programmers how different this life would be!

Don't take our word for it!

Remember, don't believe everything we're telling you. It's much more important that you approach Kabbalah like a scientific experiment. If I'm a researcher and there is a hypothesis or theory I'm trying to prove or demonstrate, I have to test that theory. When I get the same results consistently, I know I've got proof it works.

The same is true with Kabbalah. Experiment. Try the exercises. Do your Light-Work and be open to seeing if you get results. Take whatever works for you and discard the rest.

One of the beautiful things I've always appreciated about Kabbalah is that you're never going to hear the answer "because it is written."

At the same time, don't dismiss Kabbalah because it's confronting your limited thought patterns. We all have deeply ingrained belief systems. Kabbalists believe that we have to question everything and then make sure it's working for us. That's the beauty of Kabbalah: don't have blind faith. Try everything, *be open*, do the work. At the end of these twenty-three chapters, see if you haven't made a significant change in your understanding of life, in the appreciation of everything you already have, and in the excitement and newness of removing old layers of negativity. If it isn't working for you, then close this book, and give it to someone else. What's important is that you come along on this journey with us. Then, at the end, you can decide whether it was worth it or not.

I'm reminded of a story about a student of Zen Buddhism who circled the globe looking for a master. Finally, he went to the big Kahuna Zen Master and waited his turn. He was so excited; he wanted to share his practice with the Zen Master. He wanted to tell him everything he knew. As he was rambling on, the Zen Master said: "Do you want some tea?" The student said, "Yes." The master started pouring the tea. The student kept on talking. He suddenly saw that the cup was full and the Zen Master was continuing to pour. Finally, he said, "Master, the cup is full. Why do you keep on pouring?" The master said, "The cup is a lot like you. Your cup is so full of wisdom already that there is no room for anything else to go in."

We need to open ourselves up to the possibility that perhaps we've been seeing the world in a way that doesn't leave room for things as they are. Maybe we've been distracted by the way we think things should be. And possibly, if we try a different road, we may reap different results next time.

If we open ourselves up, there is an unlimited realm of possibilities. I believe that you're committed to changing whatever is not working for you. That's what guided your lists: what you want and what you don't want anymore. *I don't want any failed relationships. I don't want any more disillusionment. I want the real deal.* And the beauty is that when we open ourselves up to what Kabbalah truly offers, we can experience an unlimited sense of meaning, purpose, and happiness, which we call the Light, an important subject we will explore later in some detail.

The history of Kabbalah goes way back to the beginning of the creation of the Universe. This information was handed to us thousands of years ago and has been passed down from generation to generation to generation—through a great deal of pain and suffering so that today we don't need to suffer. Today, we don't need to hide in caves to study. We can simply decide that we want this information; we want to use its tools. You've already started the journey without any persecution, with no one preventing you, without any resistance.

So, what do you really want in life? What's limiting you? How do you prevent yourself from expanding and enjoying a bigger purpose? How do you prevent yourself from receiving more? It's time to stop throwing away the big fish. It's time to expand your capacity to catch more, to have a lot more happiness, more excitement, more meaning, a job that gives you satisfaction, not just work that pays the bills, and a relationship where you feel totally on the same page with your partner.

I suggest that you consider journaling a little every day as part of the Light-Work that I am suggesting for you. Make the effort. Make sure the desire you have to change is not only well-intentioned but also translates into effort and action. In that way, you're guaranteed to experience dramatic shifts in your life.

[Light work]

For our first Light-Work session, I'll ask you again to be very honest with yourself about what it is you need to do to create lasting fulfillment in your life. Sit down and journal on this topic for fifteen minutes. Just write. Let go. Write whatever comes to mind, and write it down as quickly as you can; don't stop until fifteen minutes is up. Get in the habit of allowing yourself to open up that channel. Whatever comes, comes. Just write it down.

Michelangelo also studied the wisdom of Kabbalah. One of his most famous pieces of work is his sculpture of David. Someone asked Michelangelo where he found the exquisite man who modeled for his sculpture. He answered, "I didn't have a model. I had no muse. I simply chipped away the excess rock and revealed what the Creator had already provided."

Start chipping away.

We all have the ability to manifest incredible happiness. We each arrive here with a magnificent Soul, but our Soul at present is covered with the dust and dirt of layers of negativity that we have accumulated. Over the course of this book, we will chip away until we remove all of our limitations and reveal our true potential.

Chapter 2
Lasting Fulfillment

Before we continue, how was the Light-Work that you did? Did you write down everything that you need to do to create lasting fulfillment? If you didn't do the Light-Work, I think it's important to stop reading and go back and do it. I want to encourage you to become accountable for the work that needs to be done. Knowledge and wisdom are not enough. Kabbalah is about living and practicing the principles every single day. And this book covers only one level of knowledge. Lasting change takes time.

It's like the story of one of the great sages, Akiva, who, at the age of forty, was one of the most negative people around, until he fell for a woman who was very spiritual. But he thought, "I can't change, so I'm never going to be good enough for her." Although they were enjoying their time together, he was convinced there was no hope. One day they walked by the bank of a river and saw a little stream passing through a big boulder. She said, "See that? Do you think the hole in that boulder, which allows the stream to pass through, happened in a day, a week, or even in a month?

No, it happened drop by drop by drop, year after year, until eventually it created the hole through the boulder allowing the water to pass."

Spiritual work through Kabbalah is the same. It doesn't happen in a day, in a week, or in a month. But eventually it penetrates. Eventually, you become a changed person. So, if one day your Light-Work doesn't get you anywhere, if it doesn't take you where you thought it would, try to remember that transformation very rarely happens overnight. It's a step-by-step process. At the end of your journey, you will be different. It may have taken you twenty, thirty, or forty years, or more to wind up in the place where you are now stuck. We have to be willing to take at least twenty or thirty or forty days to undo it.

Now, as we continue on our journey, understand that in these first few chapters there is a lot of deep information. You've already learned some of Kabbalah's history, and its tendency to expand our horizons. This information may sound a bit broad, and perhaps a bit vague, at this time. But as we progress, the information will become more specific and very personal. We will begin identifying exactly what it is that we're trying to break through.

Bear with me. We're going to get there. We've got to chip away at that rock gradually. *The keys are patience, commitment, and desire.* As long as you are willing to bring those qualities to this process, you're going to break through.

What do we desire?

You wrote about this in your Light-Work. What do you really want?

Sometimes what people think they want is very tangible. They want to lose ten pounds. They want a million dollars in the bank. They want to get married, or be in a relationship. Don't get me wrong. These are very meaningful and important things, but according to Kabbalah, what we don't realize is that we can have it ALL. We can have EVERYTHING, not just this or that.

As we've discussed, one key to having it all is desire. Thankfully, this quality is readily available. Wanting to receive is our nature.

Think of how a newborn comes into this world. What is its first instinct? It wants. It screams. It calls out to receive. If you motion your finger towards an infant, it will grab your hand. Its nature is to draw in, to take. A newborn must receive clothing, comfort, sustenance, food, and shelter. If we don't receive all those things, we simply won't make it. The problem arises when a person is twenty-seven, or thirty-eight, or forty-nine years old and still experiences the world in terms of what he or she is getting. In Kabbalah, we learn to take that desire to receive and transform it into the ability to share.

Sometimes there are situations where something good happens and we get exactly what we think we want. We get a promotion or a better job. We get married. But how long does that satisfaction last? Not very long. On the other hand, what about the time we got fired, when a project of ours failed, or when we got divorced?

The feeling of failure seems to last so much longer than our peak ecstasy moments, those "perfect" moments. Not only do we sometimes run after the wrong source of fulfillment, but even when we get it, we can't keep it. We don't take the opportunity to savor the moment, and then the moment is gone.

The real issue at hand is how strong our desire is. How deep is our commitment to what we really want? Often, it's not that deep. When you look at your life, there seem to be so many more moments of negativity and failure than happiness. We focus our desires on what we don't have–and there will always be something that we don't have. What we will learn to do here is refocus on what we want, on how we're going to get there, and how to successfully battle the obstacles that arise along the way.

Being Able to Receive

Over the years, I've counseled many couples in the months leading up to their wedding. There is so much stress in the preparation of a big wedding, and as the happy day gets closer and closer, there's more and more stress. The bride-to-be gets bronchitis; the groom-to-be gets the flu. Then, on the wedding day, the event is over in what feels like five minutes. The couple barely gets to see their friends or talk to anyone. They hardly remember the experience, which is why it's so helpful to have hundreds of photographs! It's amazing how we spend so much time planning all of the details, but it's so difficult to take it all in when it's actually happening. It is one thing to have a tremendous desire for whatever it is we want. But it's another thing altogether to allow ourselves to truly receive the fruits and fulfillment of our efforts.

Why is it so difficult to receive a compliment? Why is it so difficult for people to open up and allow real love to come in? We're so accustomed to not trusting anyone. We're so accustomed to going without and having people withhold from us. We expect disappointment; we always seem to be waiting for the other shoe to drop. It's become the human condition to spend our time waiting for that excitement and fulfillment to disappear.

Fulfillment is a very broad term, and so it's not easy to relate to. When students are trying to understand real joy and fulfillment, I suggest using a very simple litmus test: *Is this a moment you'd want to share with someone?* When you get really good news—some genuinely amazing news—what's the first thing you want to do? You want to share it with someone, right? Why? Because the essence of fulfillment is pure sharing.

If you have bad news, the last thing you want to do is share it with someone. If you've just been fired, you don't want to call everyone you know. Chances are good that if someone just told you how selfish you are, you're not going to call all your friends and repeat what you've just been told. But if someone says you have the most incredible voice and wants to sign you to a record deal, *now* you're going to call everybody.

Two kinds of desires

We all have selfish desires, but we also have the desire to give and to share with others. We have a desire to be a better listener in our relationships. We have a desire to please our kids, to do something special for them, to make them happy. When we're in love, all we want to do is please our partner by doing wonderful, sweet things for him or her. We become completely unconditional in our affections. The problem is that we can only stay in that state of unconditional giving for a short time. It's very challenging. In the beginning stages of a relationship, if I left you a message and you called me back some time later, that would not be a problem. But as I get a bit more invested and vulnerable, I begin to expect you to call me back right away. If you don't, I start to feel anxious, maybe even panicked. What happened? I started to focus on what I am receiving instead of what I am giving.

I truly believe that if we could stay in the honeymoon phase, that place of giving when we're totally in love, for five years, we would never fall out of love. It is the giving that causes the euphoria and the love.   Kabbalah explains that it is not about sharing with someone you love; it's about growing to love someone with whom you share. We would rarely have a problem in any relationship if we shared more. But what happens is that we shift our focus to: *What's in it for me? When are you going to give me attention? When are you going to spend time with me like you used to? When are you going to come up with creative things for us to do like you used to? When are you going to leave me the little surprise cards in the sock drawer like you used to?* We start dwelling on how it used to be, instead of looking at what we can do proactively to give to the other person.

When I'm in a relationship and I'm planning to take you to dinner, is my focus on how wonderful the evening will be for you? Or am I focused on how I am going to impress you so you'll like me even more? The lack of selfishness in our intentions is directly proportional to the amount of fulfillment we will receive from our efforts.

The Roots of Desire

Let's do a short exercise to be clear about the roots of our desires and their true nature. Kabbalah teaches us that our nature is built upon a desire to receive. Remember, we're built out of a desire to receive, so it's not something we need to be embarrassed about or apologize for. The problem is that receiving can turn into pure selfishness.

What's behind our actions and our attitudes? What is the nature of the energy with which we do things? What is at the core of our behavior? Let's take a closer look at ourselves as we determine the different kinds of consciousness we carry with us as we go about our lives. Consciousness is a term that means "our thoughts, desires, our belief systems, the lens through which we view the world ." What I would like you to do now in this exercise is take some time to evaluate the state of your own consciousness. It's not easy to step outside our consciousness far enough to gain any perspective on it, so we'll turn to journaling for help.

Take five minutes to write in your journal. Ask yourself: *What do I want in life? What are my goals? What is the nature of my desire? Is it really a desire to share or is it a desire to receive only for myself? What is behind my desire? Is it about my getting what I need at the expense of someone else? Or do I want others to benefit?*

Look at some of the things that you crave in life and see if you can discern the different kinds of consciousness you have in relation to them.

Innate Desire

I find it amazing how disillusioned we can become. I know that I used to have lots of dreams about what would really make me happy. A good friend of mine who's a drummer thought he wanted to be a famous musician and had fantasies of playing in front of thousands of people. Sure enough, by the time he was in his early twenties, he was playing in bands, sometimes in huge arenas. You know what? After a while, every tour that he went on, every downtown that he visited in America looked the same. Every hotel room at the end of the day looked identical. He had people screaming his name when he was on stage; then, when the lights went out, people went home and he was left feeling empty and alone. An incredible sense of disillusionment sometimes accompanies all the stimulation that comes with that type of lifestyle.

It's incredible how something we think is going to give us so much excitement can burn out so quickly. It's like a light bulb that blows its circuits—even if it's just a little fifteen-watt light bulb in a fridge. You open the door and the bulb blows. For a split second, you get that flash of incredible light, much greater than the fifteen watts. Then it's suddenly dark. This is a perfect metaphor for what we believe we're going to get in life. We think, *Wow!* We're going to get all this incredible stuff. We're going to get this promotion; we're going to earn more money; we're going to move into our dream home; we're going to get this new car. When we get what we think we want, the light burns bright for a moment. But then the feeling starts to fade.

We can't take anything with us when we die. What we take when we walk down the street is who we are. It's not our bank account or our status or power. If you're not good enough without it, you'll never be good enough with it. According to Kabbalah, who I am in the world is really the sum total of everything that I've shared with others. Once we start to understand this and actually live this way it is very liberating.

Refining Our Desires

There is a story of two tourists who go to Acapulco in Mexico and see these two Mexican fisherman. One of the tourists goes over and asks: "What do you do all day?"

They say, "Well, we fish all day. That's all we do. We have a little hut. We live there and we fish all day."

The tourists ask, "Why don't you get a job? Actually do something for a living?"

The fishermen talk about it to each other in Spanish, then say: "What would that job offer us at the end of the day?"

"If you get a job, you can make some money. Maybe you could buy a decent house."

They think that over. "Okay, after I have this house and this job, what else do I do?"

"If you work hard enough, potentially you could start your own company and be in charge of other people. Then you could have a large corporation. You could travel from place to place and see the world."

"Very interesting. And, then what?"

"Well, then you would have enough money to buy your own island, and you could sit on the beach in the sunshine and fish all day."

The point is that merely increasing our desire doesn't necessarily increase our fulfillment. We need to know not only that we want more out of life, but we also need to know what that more is exactly. And it's not just one thing that will give us fulfillment. We want to enjoy every aspect of our life. That's real fulfillment. Real fulfillment doesn't come at the expense of something else. Real fulfillment is not working late every night to earn a million bucks but neglecting our family in the process. We have to get to a point when we say: "I want all of this to work." Through Kabbalah, we have the tools to combat the difficulties, increase the Light, and gain real fulfillment in every area of our life.

Buddha spent half of his life studying and learning every bit of universal wisdom made available to him, so that during the second part of his life, he was simply outputting this wisdom. He shared the information with anyone who sought answers. Again, his desire to receive wisdom for himself was merely a preamble to the second part of his life when he shared unselfishly. When we talk about our desires and fulfillment, there is nothing wrong with a bit of selfishness, as long as our desire is real, and, in the big picture, it will bring real fulfillment to us and those around us.

There is a wonderful story about a man who leaves the world and arrives at the pearly gates, where he is given a preview of heaven and hell. Both scenarios have the exact same setting: people sitting around a huge pot of stew, each holding a wooden spoon with a very long handle. In Hell, he sees emaciated people trying to feed themselves, but try as they might, they're not able to get the food into their mouths using the cumbersome spoons. In Heaven, on the other hand, the people look healthy, with nice, rosy complexions. The difference is that in Heaven, they're feeding each other using their long spoons. They're sharing, because they understand that the only way they can eat, have the real fulfillment and sustenance that they need, is by taking care of one another.

So, what is Hell? Hell is not having the ability to share with others.

Creating Our Lives

I once was fortunate enough to see the difference between managing and leading: a manager gets people to *do* things, while a leader gets people to *become* something. In Kabbalah, our life is about becoming; it's about taking the lead in our own life. It's not about merely surviving or enduring. There is very little energy in that.

Life is about fulfillment. It's not about *who* we are, but rather *how* we are: how we're showing up in life, how we're being in our relationships—that's what's going to determine the quality of our fulfillment. It's about creating our life and being the cause of our own reality.

Yes, we are the creators of our reality.

If our reality is in any way unsatisfying, chaotic or stuck, there is no one we can blame. Nothing is happening to us. If we're not satisfied, we have caused the limitation. We have to understand what it means to create the movie of our life.

[Light-Work]

Turn to a new page in your journal and write down some of the differences that you've discovered between temporary and lasting fulfillment. Think about the short-term solutions we use to satisfy our desires versus the lasting solutions that help us to see the bigger picture. What is the difference between thriving and surviving, between accomplishing and coping? What desires give you lasting rather than temporary fulfillment? What motivates you to sort out the difference, and how will you benefit spiritually from this process? In other words, how does your spiritual growth benefit you?

Remember, as with Michelangelo's sculpture of David, our purpose every day is to chip away until we get deeper and deeper to the true Light of fulfillment that exists in each of us.

Chapter 3
Your Purpose

Our journey continues.

Check over your Light-Work in which you looked at the different kinds of fulfillment—temporary fulfillment or lasting fulfillment—that we accomplish with our actions. What's the difference? Our focus with Kabbalah is lasting fulfillment; we want the deep stuff.

In our search for the deep stuff, one of the things that we will undoubtedly discover is that we all have blind spots or blockages; we might call them character defects, limitations or inhibitions. Whatever we call them, we get stuck sometimes. That's why we're here—to repair or correct our limitations. That's the purpose of this lifetime. We each have corrections to make along the way in order to get back on track. But there is also a big-picture reason why we came here to this physical world. And it goes beyond the search for personal fulfillment.

A Giant Jigsaw Puzzle

Each of us represents one of the pieces of a giant jigsaw puzzle. These pieces come in all different sizes, shapes, colors, and textures, but at the end of the day, every single piece is crucial to the complete picture. It's a bit like a karmic Humpty Dumpty—we've got to put all these pieces back together again. That's part of correcting the original pattern that was designed for us. In Kabbalah, we use the term *Tikkun*, which means correction. This is a deep concept because it addresses one of the deepest questions we have to answer: *Why am I here? What's my purpose?*

Just understanding that there is a broader purpose is bringing us closer to finding our solution. There's a Chinese proverb that says: "If you don't know where you're going, you're never going to get there." It reminds me of the person who went to the kabbalist and said: "I'm so lost. I'm so off the path." And the kabbalist told him: "If you're looking for the path, you're already on the path."

Along our path each and every one of us will uncover both garbage and gifts—stuff we're naturally good at and stuff we're naturally bad at. I was born with the gift of Attention Deficit Disorder and have gone through life with ADD. You would think that something like that would be my garbage, something that would stop me along my path. Instead, by the age of 33, I've written a number of books and created numerous products—because I had to. I couldn't do just one thing; I had to do fifty things.

We have to find the Light somewhere in our garbage. That's where our Light is hiding. We may not know what our garbage is—or what our gifts are—right now. In fact, I didn't find out about my ADD until a few years ago. But when we start identifying the gifts and the garbage in our lives, they will eventually lead us to our divine purpose.

Kabbalah & Astrology

Kabbalah talks a great deal about astrology, although not in the same way the columns you read in magazines or the daily newspaper might. We've all read those blurbs under our astrological sign. "You will meet a special friend this week," they say. But that's not real astrology, and in our hearts we know that. Kabbalistic astrology goes back 4,000 years to the time when Abraham, one of the original kabbalists, named each of the signs of the constellations and explained their meaning.

Now why did he do that?

He gave us this information so we could understand the influence of the sign under which we were born and, more importantly, learn how not to be controlled by that influence. What's the point in coming into this world if you will be told, as a Scorpio, that you're a control freak and that's your designated lot in life? Who wants to stay a control freak? Or, you're a Cancer, and therefore you're likely to be depressed and moody your whole life. What kind of life is that? Kabbalah teaches us that the reason you need to know the limitations and the highest potential of each of those signs is so we can transform the negative into good and make the most of the positive attributes that we have.

I'll give you a couple of examples. In Kabbalah, we talk about an idea known as the Libran Complex. Typically, those born under the zodiac sign of Libra seek harmony; they want to balance the scales. Why? Because they want everyone to be happy. They're sharing, kind, thoughtful, sensitive people. They come here into this life seemingly without baggage. So, what's the problem? The problem is that we don't come here to be nice, kind people. We come to this world—every one of us—to transform our nature, to correct whatever aspect of our nature is selfish, blocked, and limited, so that we can experience true, lasting fulfillment.

Why would a Libra come here? What does a Libra need to change?

Librans need to go against their nature and establish boundaries, to risk not having others approve of what they think, to go against the popular view, to have people get mad at them and be okay with that, to say no, and to not be walked all over. These are tremendously difficult changes for a Libran, but they're essential for maintaining human dignity and respect.

Let's pretend for a moment that a kid approaches his Libra father and asks: "Dad, can I have a hundred bucks to get some cocaine on the street corner?" We wouldn't want the father to respond with: "Absolutely! No problem. Whatever makes you happy." Clearly, such a person would not have their spiritual house in order. Most fathers would say something along the lines of: "Absolutely not! Are you crazy?" because they recognize the need for establishing healthy limits with their children. Establishing limits is difficult for most Librans, because it means that the person on the receiving end might end up unhappy. But that is the skill they are here to develop.

If you're a Cancer and tend to be overly sensitive and moody, your task in life is to look at how your actions are affecting others, instead of focusing on your own sensitivities and how others affect you. That is the purpose of our astrological signs—to encourage us to change whatever aspect of our personality is not in synch with the Light.

What Is Best for the Greatest Good?

Real change requires interacting with other people in our environment. We can't do this transformation alone in a cave and expect any real change. Transformation includes the component of other people—influencing them, helping them, and sharing with them. Yes, we need to find what in ourselves we need to change, but the work extends beyond our individual selves.

Take for example the Dalai Lama, who had to flee Tibet when it was overrun by China. He could have relocated somewhere luxurious and enjoyed the privileges of his rank. But, instead of giving up his work, the Dalai Lama rededicated himself to his people, and he continues to provide leadership to Tibetans around the world from his home in India. He has even found the strength to feel compassion for the people who ousted him. He could have spent his life feeling angry, frustrated, and resentful. Instead, he let go. And he has become one of the most sharing individuals on the planet.

That's real change—directing positive energy toward someone who has harmed you. It reminds me of the Amish community in Pennsylvania where five schoolchildren were gunned down in their one-room schoolhouse. Instead of choosing hate and resentment, the Amish community extended its love and forgiveness to the family of the man who murdered their children.

At the end of the day, you realize that those who have harmed you are acting out their *own* movie, and you don't have to include that negativity in *your* movie. Even ignoring these people keeps them as much in your movie as if they're playing an active part. To extend good will to someone who has harmed you, on the other hand, actually removes that person from your movie. So the Dalai Lama was strong enough to take the Chinese leaders out of his movie, just as the Amish were strong enough to remove the killer from theirs.

If you look at people who have chosen to make a change in themselves, you'll see that such change always included the good of other people. The movie *Coach Carter* is based on the true story of a high school coach, who closed down the gym because his students did not perform well academically. The parents were outraged. They wanted to remove the coach, who responded by saying: "You don't have to fire me. If it's like this, I quit." When the coach went to the gym to collect his things, he saw the students doing their homework. They said to him, "They can fire you, but they can't make us play basketball." In that moment, he felt true fulfillment. He saw firsthand that he had made a difference to those kids. The point is this: others are inherently involved in our growth.

How many rock stars have you heard about whose lives were ruined by drugs or alcohol? The richer they got, the more chaos came into their lives. It's very sad. On the other hand, look at the singer Bono from the hugely successful band U2. He was named Man of the Year by *Time* magazine for his philanthropic work in Africa, helping to alleviate hunger and preventable diseases. Thirty thousand people a day die there from diseases that could easily be prevented. This shocking reality inspired Bono to take a break from making music—from making money—in order to make a difference in the lives of others. The same is true for Madonna, who took time out from her very busy life to write educational books for children and dedicate herself to helping orphans in Africa.

Do you know how many hugely successful businessmen and women I've talked to who feel they have nothing? They feel literally empty inside. One forty-year-old, self-made man who came to see me was probably worth a hundred million dollars, and he had worked really hard to get there. He lived in a compound in Malibu, California that was built like a fortress, with walls around it and a shark aquarium. Can you imagine sitting at home watching a shark swim around your living room? But the guy didn't trust a Soul. He was probably one of the most fearful controlling people I've ever met. He wouldn't let anyone into his life, yet he was telling me how lonely he felt. All because he had never developed the ability to share his love and abundance with others.

When one of our teachers first came to Los Angeles in the early 1980s from England, he met some teens who had just graduated from Beverly Hills High School. Their parents were enormously affluent and had given their children everything, from the best education to their own BMWs at age sixteen. Now what did these teens have to look forward to? What did they have to aspire to? These educated teens were dealing drugs, dropping out of school; they were angry and belligerent. What happened to make these teens, who had everything, feel as if they had nothing? I believe their sense of entitlement had undermined their sense of being able to contribute to this world.

One of my favorite quotes is, "Expecting life to treat you well because you are a good person is a bit like expecting an angry bull not to charge because you are a vegetarian." This is genius! We have to be prepared for life, which means we have to be willing and able to face the fact that it will be challenging. Nothing will be handed to us on the proverbial silver platter. We are here to overcome our limited nature, not to be afraid of change, but to embrace it.

You'll know that you have begun your journey when it starts becoming difficult. If it's too easy, you're not heading in the right direction. If you're doing a Light-Work exercise or one of the other exercises and think: "Oh, this is a piece of cake," then I encourage you to try harder, so you can get out of your comfort zone.

If our purpose in life is to change our natures, to repair and correct our limitations, and to overcome the selfish aspects of ourselves, the question is this: As intelligent, educated, aware people, why do we make the same mistakes over and over? Why do we still get stuck? Why do we still choose to go against our better judgment?

Blind Spots

One of the definitions of addiction from a clinical perspective is to continue to abuse substances, act out, or be self-destructive, while fully understanding the negative consequences of those actions. Let's take smoking, for example. Every time you take out a cigarette, it tells you right there on the pack that smoking causes emphysema, lung cancer, and birth defects. But your addiction pushes you to override the warning, and you find yourself saying for the one hundredth time: "Yeah, I know it's bad. But I'll quit tomorrow."

It's as if we don't see or we choose not to see the roadblocks we put in our own way. This blind spot is the part of ourselves that we can't access. In Kabbalah, we have a code word for this blind spot—it's called *Satan*. Another word for it is *ego*.

When we look back at the history of the word *Satan*, we discover that it's an old English term that comes from an older Greek word meaning *adversary*, or "our other side." It's not the little red man with the pitchfork that we all imagine. It's our real Opponent—a force in this world that is actively blinding us. It's the force that makes us forget to appreciate our gifts, encourages us to feel entitled, and implants unhealthy thoughts inside our brain.

Why are we so unconscious of our blind spots? Why do we seek out such destructive behavior despite knowing exactly what's coming? Why do we make such foolish decisions even though we fully appreciate the consequences of our actions? Once again, our blind spots, once they're slightly redirected, will turn out to be the pathways to our gifts.

A ticket to ride

We wouldn't get on a plane without looking at the boarding pass. We're very specific about our travel itineraries. We know exactly where we're headed when we book a flight. We don't want to be shocked by landing at the wrong destination. In the same way, we need to be clear about where we're headed on our present journey.

To this end, let's do a visualization exercise together. I ask that for now, please, take a few minutes to close your eyes and relax. Shut off any distractions and focus inward, because we have a very important job to do. The goal of this visualization is to find out how exactly we are off-track and where we need to focus our attention in order to remove any blockages to our spiritual progress. Find somewhere quiet to sit and take a couple of slow, deep breaths in through your mouth and out through your nose. Think about the fact that your life has a purpose. You're on a mission here. Your Soul has brought you to this world to accomplish something quite important and very specific. There is only one thing preventing you from accomplishing your mission: your ego. Your ego is your fear, your insecurity, your doubt, your blind spots. And you can't see why you keep causing the same problems over and over again. You don't recognize how your selfishness is causing other people to be upset with you, reject you, or avoid you. In order to get past your ego, beyond the superficial aspects of who you are, beyond your *persona*, you'll need to find the courage to dig deep. When you go far beneath the surface, you'll find yourself in a place where there is no ego. All that exists is your relationship with God.

Kabbalah teaches us that if you want to know the nature of your relationship with God, examine how you are when it's just you and the Creator and no one else is looking. When there is no one to impress. When there is no one to admire you. When it's just you and the Creator. You and your Higher Power. You and the Light. Do you have integrity? Do you have an open dialogue? Is there a give and take? Do you feel alone, cut off, and disconnected? What kind of relationship do you have with God? The degree to which we have a true, close relationship with the Creator—whatever that may mean to us—is equal to the degree that we are unblocked, open, and connected with the rest of the world. Our blind spots need to be brought to light before they can be of benefit to us and others. We need to remove those layers that prevent us from true happiness. In order to achieve this, we'll need to do a little excavation.

You might find yourself thinking: "I'm ambivalent. My energy is low. I'm confused. It doesn't mean my life is not working in some areas, but the truth is that I don't have true happiness. I don't have any sense of excitement or passion." Getting to this place of honesty will prepare us for the real work, which is to discover the limiting beliefs and thought patterns about who we are and what we're capable of. Those unconscious emotions and memories that we have collected and held onto from prior experiences are the source of our frustration, pain, or lack of trust. As you dig, have the courage to look around. What do you see?

It's just you and the Creator. If you listen, the Creator is trying to show you exactly what it is you need to repair. When you can pinpoint that the knocking sound is in the engine of a car, you can diagnose and fix the problem. But if we keep driving a car that is in need of repair, with no clue that there is even any damage, we cause much greater harm in the long run. Kabbalah is intended to be preventive—we want to prevent ourselves from causing chaos. In its place, we aim to create joy.

Imagine, as with Michelangelo's sculpture of David, that you've got a hammer in one hand and a chisel in the other. Gently start chipping away at the limitations, fears, and the self-defeating voice in your head that keeps you from fulfillment. Rid yourself of that unrelenting self-esteem issue. Let go of the baggage. Just put the suitcases down. Imagine the sense of freedom that you'll have.

Just as a hot air balloon rises in the air when you throw the sand-bags over the side, you, too, will be elevated. Take a few moments to consider those things that you haven't looked at closely before. I know that we are all busy people. But it's time to slow down for a few minutes and take a look. What you're about to discover will excite you. It's nothing to be afraid of. But if you don't look, you'll never find anything.

Here are some specific questions you can ask yourself to begin this process: *Why do I have such fear? Why can't I let love in? Why am I so convinced that the people in my life can't be trusted? Why am I so convinced that I'm no good? Where does this information come from? Why am I so angry? Why do I feel numb? What has happened that has caused me to feel so shut off from God and from my inner self? How did I become so skeptical and afraid?*

It might feel scary to ask these questions and to hear what comes up. But one of our first steps in having the courage to change is to allow ourselves to hear the answers to these questions. Soon, you will recognize the outmoded beliefs and behaviors that are keeping you stuck. When you finish considering these questions, go to your journal and write down your list of limitations—your blind spots, your blockages, and whatever else you found. You'll be surprised what happens when you ask for clarity and are willing to listen.

[Light-Work]

Imagine seeing yourself on a giant, plasma TV screen. You're watching your life; seeing yourself acting from a blind spot; seeing the fear grabbing hold of you; seeing the anger come out; seeing yourself shrinking away in fear and rejection.

Now imagine that you're holding a remote control in your hand. Every time you "see" yourself about to enter another blind spot, simply click the Pause button. Wait a minute. Stop. Freeze frame. Now ask yourself: *Do I really want to say what's about to come out of my mouth? Is it going to serve the greater good? As much as I feel vindicated in yelling at this person right now, is it really going to bring about happiness and fulfillment? Or, is it going to cause me even more chaos and destruction in the long run?*

For your Light work, imagine you're watching yourself. Become an observer of your life. Every time you find yourself heading towards that blind spot, hit the pause button, and ask yourself the questions above. Wake up! We don't want to sleepwalk through our lives. If we don't recognize when we are about to emotionally sabotage ourselves and others, how are we supposed to change our actions?

Here is a k-Tool that you can use: I call it the proactive formula.

1. **Stop.** Hit the pause button when you find yourself becoming stuck in a blind spot.
2. Ask yourself: **What am I doing?** Is this really how I want to be acting?
3. Celebrate the fact that you've identified the problem. **You've just gotten to the seed level of your blind spot.**
4. Ask yourself: What else can I do? **How can I handle this situation differently?** Acknowledge that there are other choices you can make; there are other options.

These steps can help you begin to correct destructive patterns that you may have had your entire life. Now, after pausing and considering your actions, you might discover that the situation is so overwhelming that there is nothing else you can do but move forward with your actions. And that is okay. This is not about fixing anything right now. Just give yourself the opportunity to hit that pause button and stop. As we continue, you'll have more tools for handling such situations. These are everyday tools that are going to enable you to gain clarity, and take control of your life.

Chapter 4

Creating Fulfillment

How did you do with your Light-Work? Did you have an opportunity to use the k-Tool, The Proactive Formula that we provided? Were you able to successfully stop when you started to be reactive or selfish? Were you able to grab the remote control and pause yourself in that negative action, take control, identify what was going on, and ask yourself the question: *What am I doing?*

Remember, just by asking yourself the question, by identifying and stopping that potentially negative act, you're already one step ahead of the game. You should feel good about that.

This chapter is going to help us understand how we create our own opportunities and fulfillment. We're now going to begin the real work of Kabbalah, the real work of spiritual transformation.

Earning Our Fulfillment

Kabbalists explain to us that fulfillment, if it's going to last, has to be earned by us. Fulfillment cannot be handed to us on a plate; we have to make the effort to bring it into our existence. This notion is fundamental to transformation. It comes from a Universal Law known as The Law of Affinity.

Affinity means attraction. It means *like attracts like.*

As we said earlier, our inherent nature when we come into this world is to be a receiving vessel, like a newborn that needs to receive until he or she becomes full. Yet the essence of true fulfillment, which comes from the Light of the Creator, is purely to share.

This puts us in an interesting situation. On the one hand, we desire true fulfillment, which comes from this incredible energy of sharing. On the other hand, our nature is the energy of receiving. So, it's a paradox. Fortunately, The Law of Affinity tells us exactly how to negotiate these two energies.

If you directly connect to the Light of the Creator without any filtering of this Light, you're going to receive an instant shot of blinding energy, followed by burnout. It's like a light bulb whose filament breaks; there is a flash of light, then darkness. Our life's purpose, quite simply, is to learn how to activate our sharing nature so we have more affinity with the Light. When we are more like the Light of the Creator, our fulfillment burns long and bright. There is no impending darkness.

Remember, we must earn the fulfillment that we bring into our lives, which means we have to get outside of our comfort-seeking selfish nature. My father, Rav Berg, tells a story that illustrates this point.

There once was a man who spent his whole life robbing banks and stealing money from other people. He was a criminal genius who could easily break through the most sophisticated security systems. When he died, an angel greeted him. The man thought, "Wow, this is a great place! There's food; there's a spa. Nice sleeping accommodations. There's everything I could ever need!" But eventually he became a bit bored. He said, "Angel, can you help me? I would like to rob a bank."

The angel said, "Sure. Which bank would you like to rob?'

"You see that bank on the corner? That's the one I want to hit."

"What time would you like to do so?"

"Three in the afternoon."

"How much money would you like in the safe?"

"Two million."

"Perfect, two million dollars will be there waiting for you. Here are the plans of the bank layout. Just walk in and take it."

The man said, "No, no, no, no. You don't understand. I want to plan this. I want to make sure that I bypass the alarms and security on my own."

"No, no. You can't do that," the angel told him. "Now that you've died, things are a little different. You just tell us what you want and we provide it for you."

"But I'm the greatest bank robber the world has ever known. There is no excitement in doing it like this. What kind of heaven is this?"

The angel looked at him gravely and replied: "Who said this is heaven?"

Satisfaction comes from overcoming a challenge and earning the sense of accomplishment that results. When we don't feel challenged or feel any sense of having earned something, we move towards chaos. But when we earn, overcome, or change an aspect of ourselves for the better, we experience the heavenly energy of Light.

A while ago a friend I hadn't seen in a while came into Los Angeles, called me and said: "Listen, I would love to take you to lunch on Friday. Pick any restaurant you want." I said, "Great, let's go to the Ivy." The Ivy is a swanky, fantastic restaurant in Los Angeles. We went to the Ivy and had the most amazing lunch— five courses of the best food in town, with a fabulous ambiance, to boot. The bill came and, of course, I offered to pay. He immediately said, "No, no, please. I want to take care of this." It was a really nice gesture; it was great to see him and to enjoy such a fabulous lunch.

The following week, he called and said: "I'm coming into town again. Let's go to that Ivy place; it was great."

"Great! I'll pick up the tab this time."

"No, no, no. When I move here, eventually, you can take me, but I want to take you again."

Sure enough, on Friday afternoon we went to lunch. We experienced more of the most amazing food and fabulous ambiance. The bill came and I wrestled with him to let me pay, which he adamantly refused.

This went on for weeks. He would come into town and take me to the same wonderful restaurant. I was becoming a little bit frustrated. In fact, I was starting to feel resentful and I wasn't even enjoying the food anymore. In fact, I wanted to avoid my friend all together.

Wait a minute! What was going on here? I was being treated to the most satisfying restaurant in town by a generous and successful friend, who had absolutely nothing up his sleeve. He simply wanted to share. He valued our relationship and wanted to show it, but I was feeling trapped. It made no sense. How could it be that I was getting everything I wanted, yet I was feeling unhappy and bitter?

It's like the Beverly Hills High School brat who has been indulged and spoiled by his parents his entire life. You would think that a kid who has everything—the best education, the most amazing clothes, the best cars—would be successful when he grows up. Instead, he grows up rebellious, angry, sporting blue hair, and dealing drugs. What's happening here? Despite getting every-thing he could ever want, he's not happy. He's not fulfilled.

According to Kabbalah this is a very significant paradox. It has nothing to do with overly indulgent parenting or a friend who wants to take you to lunch. It's a phenomenon that occurs when we receive fulfillment without having earned it for ourselves. That unearned fulfillment leaves us feeling empty and uncomfortable, and the high of having had our wants fulfilled is even briefer than usual.

When I wrote the book *True Prosperity* about business and Kabbalah, I did some research on lottery winners. One would assume that when people win $100 million, even $50 million, they're set for the rest of their lives and should be happy. Yet an actual study shows that lottery winners are miserable. Some have lost their money. Some have lost their families. Some have lost everything. Some commit suicide. Winning the lottery gave them a shot of energy, a blast of light, a giant influx of money. But hav-ing earned none of it, they didn't know how to handle it.

Imagine you're a trust fund baby. You never have to work, but you never experience fulfillment either. When everything is provided to you, you have no motivation, no desire. If there is no need to earn money, why should you go to work? Why not sit at home, play

Xbox, watch TV, and hang out. What's the point? As a result, you never learn what it means to create fulfillment on your own, you never develop your gifts, or find your purpose in life.

Imagine that you've been handed a golden golf club by Tiger Woods. It's magical; every ball you hit with this club becomes an instant hole-in-one, every time. You're going to be a very famous gold player, which will be exciting, at least for a while. But the golf starts to become boring. Hole-in-one after hole-in-one. There is no challenge, and it's not your skill that leads to success: it's just the club.

Or imagine being an incredible chess player. You're smart. You figure out all the moves. You start playing against amateur 16-year-old kids who barely know the game. You're destroying them, game after game. Again, you become bored. Where is the challenge? Then along comes a kid who is an incredible chess genius and he wins a game against you. Now you're interested; now you're excited. Now you are engaged. Why? Now you have a challenge to overcome.

Imagine buying your Ph.D. On the one hand, it would certainly be more convenient, but a sense of accomplishment isn't included in the purchase price. That only comes when you put your body and Soul into it, when you give it your blood, sweat, and tears. If you could simply buy your doctorate, there would be no real value in it.

That's why we enjoy watching sports. We love sports figures, because we never know if they're going to make the shot or not.

If Michael Jordan made every shot and his team won every game, it would be boring. Sports would become dull. Wayne Gretzky on the ice is another great example. He earned his greatness by failing sometimes.

One of my friends was a psychotherapist specializing in family relations when he began to study Kabbalah seriously. In his own life he had an unfulfilling pattern of relationships with women. His relationships never went anywhere. Either he was choosing women who were not quite over a past relationship, or he was in the mode of rescuing the women he was dating. He learned something profound from Kabbalah that years of therapy had never made clear: he genuinely wanted to help someone who was stuck, in pain, or lost. He experienced satisfaction in being the knight in shining armor, by coming in and saving the day.

However, he noticed that the more he tried to save these women from an addiction, drugs, ex-boyfriend, financial debt, or whatever their struggle was, the more resentful and withholding they became. The more he tried to rescue them, the angrier they became. This made absolutely no sense to him. He figured they were nuts.

What he discovered through Kabbalah was that he could blame them all he wanted, but who was picking the women? They weren't exactly forcing themselves on him. The reason it wasn't working out is because he was giving them no opportunity to grow in the relationship. His rescuing was crowding out any chance for them to step into the relationship and earn his trust and respect.

This idea of earning our fulfillment, which I call *earnership*, works on both sides of the spectrum. We can be the indulged, but we can also be the indulger, which is just as dangerous. We can be the ones who are being spoiled like the trust fund kid, or we can be the guy who falls in love after two dates and sends flowers to his new crush every day. Remember that Universal Law does not allow for coercion. There has to be a give *and* take in relationships. There has to be sharing and receiving in order to get to a place of trust and unity. We can't demand trust and respect and expect to get it. We have to earn it, just like we have to earn our fulfillment.

The 1 Percent and the 99 Percent

When we can see into blind spots we can get the bigger picture. We can see how everything fits together. The kabbalists talk a great deal about the big picture, because it is where fulfillment comes from.

Kabbalists give us code words to explain two realities that coexist: the 1 Percent refers to physical reality as we see and experience it with our five senses. Physicists tell us that if we look at an atom under the microscope, only one percent of it is physical. The rest is empty space. Kabbalists refer to this portion of our Universe as the 99 Percent. And that's what we are trying to connect to—the 99 Percent world—in order to receive that energy or fulfillment. That's what we have to earn. The question is: How do we tap into this realm? How do we really earn the Light?

Take the example of the Red String I mentioned earlier in this book. Kabbalistically, it's not just a Red String. The actual string is the 1 Percent. Its energy, meaning, and power are from the 99 Percent because of the energy that is imbued in it when we meditate on it at the tomb of Rachel, who is considered by Kabbalah to be the conduit for the energy of protection in this world. We actually bring every piece of Red String to her tomb in Hebron and meditate on it there. That energy and light is the 99 percent of the Red String. All the mystical tools in Kabbalah are a part of the 99 Percent. When I give you Light-Work to do, it's working on the 99 Percent, on the concealed level of your reality.

Much of what we study and experience here in this book works on the hidden level. When we talk about temporary fulfillment and permanent fulfillment, temporary fulfillment always comes from the level of the 1 Percent, while permanent fulfillment comes from the 99 Percent level. Earning is the elevator that takes us from the 1 Percent level all the way up to the 99 Percent level.

When you look at someone's brain, you can't see the mind. A thought is not physical, consciousness is not physical. It's an energy, an idea. For example, if we were going to build a tree house, what would be our first step? It would be a thought like, *Let's go build a tree house.* This idea is not physical. It's consciousness.

Medical researchers conducted a study in which one group of cancer patients had people who meditated on their well-being while they went through treatment, while another group of similar patients didn't have anyone meditating for them. Otherwise they all followed the same course of treatment. The results? The incidence of recovery and healing was fifty percent greater in the group that had people meditating on them. Consciousness, which is not physical and tangible, connects directly to physical outcomes.

This is an idea that quantum physicists helped explain by analyzing sub-atomic parts and energy fields. We know now that just because we can't see energy, does not mean that it does not have profound effects. Everything we do is connected to everything around us. My thoughts are in some way affecting you and the energy around you, even though these thoughts are not physical. That's the 99 Percent at work. Obviously, if I hit you, push you, or steal from you, I'm talking about a 1 Percent impact. But we can also have a tremendous impact, positive or negative, in the realm of the non-physical.

[Exercise]

Think of something that you're proud of in your relationships, your work, your career, or even in your childhood. Now ask yourself, *Did I earn that? Did I put much effort into it or was it handed to me?*

One of our teachers tells the story of how he completed his thesis for his master's degree; these were probably the most difficult months of his life. This was a time when very few people had word processors or computers, and he didn't know how to type. He literally had to write the paper in pencil and scramble to get a friend who had a computer to type it up. He schlepped to Manhattan Beach from L.A. and spent day after day at a friend's apartment with no air-conditioning. He had to get this thesis done or he wasn't going to graduate. He was drinking tons of coffee so he wouldn't fall asleep. When he turned that paper in and finally got his master's degree, it was one of the most memorable days of his life. Twenty years later, he still feels a sense of accomplishment. He deserved it. He earned it. Imagine what it would be like if he had bought that thesis. Would he have the same feeling? I don't think so.

Think of something you're proud of. I guarantee you that it's something you *earned*. As Abraham Lincoln said, "I'm not bound to win. I'm bound to be true. I'm not bound to succeed, but I'm bound to live up to the light that I have." We feel proud when we have lived up to our potential through earnership.

[K-Tool: Restriction]

One essential k-Tool is learning how to take control of our actions. This idea is so crucial, in fact, that when we define spirituality according to Kabbalah, we say it means "to have absolute responsibility and control over our thoughts, feelings, and actions." We achieve this through *free will*—the ability to determine the actions we take, the words and gestures we use, and the feelings we express or don't express. In Kabbalah, the tool that enables us to control these reactions is known as *restriction*—learning how to control our ego, learning how to control our selfish tendencies.

The simplest way to understand restriction is through the model of the light bulb. A light bulb has three components: the positive charge; the negative charge; and the crucial element in between these positive and negative charges, known as the filament. Its function is to limit how much energy is drawn. Like a light bulb, we as human beings can't receive all the juice at once. It's a bit like putting your finger directly into an electric socket; that would be way too much juice! Or, plugging a hairdryer into a power station—you'd get fried. But does this mean that electricity is bad? No, not at all. Without it we couldn't live the lives we do. But without some regulation, there's too much juice coming in at one time. The energy output has to be brought down a notch. It has to be reduced to a manageable level.

That's what the tool of restriction is about. It's not about telling ourselves: "I don't want to receive." Sure we do. Instead, it's about not trying to receive everything all at once. I'll give you a simple example. I love chocolate, chocolate cake in particular. I realize that after I've had two pieces of chocolate cake, it's time to put on the brakes, because I'm going to have a headache if I continue eating. For now, two pieces is enough. Restriction doesn't mean that I have to stop liking chocolate cake. Come on, I love chocolate! I'm not repressing or shutting off my desire for chocolate cake, but I am choosing to limit how much I'm taking in.

In other words, we all want energy. That's one of the first Universal Laws. We all are driven to receive lasting fulfillment. But it's important to make sure we don't draw too much at one time. It's a bit like a sponge that becomes saturated and can't absorb any more water. Despite its saturated state, the function of the sponge remains the same.

If I try to get too much attention, if I try to be the one that everybody has to listen to, if I love to hear myself speak, I'm bound to cause conflict around me, because people will become sick of me. I need to say to myself: "You know what? It's time to stop speaking." In this way, I control my need for attention, that tendency to make everything all about me. This is a crucial relationship skill. It's our nature to want to take for ourselves, yet we need to learn how to control how much we are taking.

One of the first rules in Kabbalah is this: *always take the harder route*. Whichever is harder for you to restrict, bingo! That's the one you need to restrict. The ones that are easy aren't our true battles. We're truly practicing restriction, lowering the electrical current, when we're doing something that's not easy for us to do.

Now, restriction does not mean repression. It does not mean I'm going to shove my feelings under the rug. For example, if my buttons get pushed, I get angry. I'm not going to act like I'm not angry and go into denial. Restriction means saying to yourself: *I know I'm so mad that I'm probably going to say something that I'm going to regret later, so right now I'm going to take a little time out. I'm going to use my k-Tool and hit the pause button and hold on a minute. Let me gather myself. How do I want to handle this? I'm still angry. I'm upset. I need to talk to you about something that you've done.*

If I come from a place of explosive rage, there's no way I will create fulfillment with my actions. It may be important to express what I'm angry about, but I need to do it by being in control. I might need to be assertive by saying: "Listen, I need to talk to you about something. I'm upset with what you did and I need to express it. I would like you to understand where I'm coming from. Did I misunderstand something?" We do this instead of ripping someone's head off, which is not a kabbalistic behavior!

[Light-Work]

Let's get to the work we need to do to truly understand this principle called restriction. Go back to the very first thing we asked you to do in chapter one, which was to think about what you really want from life. You are building your arsenal of tools now, which will help you to keep chipping away. Remember, we're on this excavation together. Surely, if we dig six or seven feet down, we will find something different than we found when we were barely scratching the surface. What is it you're truly after? Have you gotten to a place where you can see that money, material possessions, your parents' approval, the perfect body, or celebrity status won't bring you fulfillment? No? Then, keep digging. Then write your thoughts down in your journal.

Cause
& Effect

Chapter 5
Choice

We're starting to get a clearer understanding of what it is we genuinely want, what it is that's evading us, and what will bring us more lasting, meaningful fulfillment. If you have not done the Light-Work, please go back and do it. There are no shortcuts in this system. Remember, that's one of the principles of earnership. Now that you understand this concept, let's talk about choice. Did you know that we each have the opportunity—and the responsibility—to create our own reality? Yes, our reality is fully determined by the choices we make.

Cause & Effect

When we come into this world as newborns, we do not make any choices. As a child, our choices continue to be limited. As teenagers, we either rebel against our parents or we follow their instructions because we don't want to be cut off from the family tree. Within this framework, we are playing a very small role in the creation our own experience.

This is what the Opponent, Satan, wants—he wants us to be reactors *to* and not creators *of* our life experiences. As we grow in life, we're bombarded by TV ads for designer jeans and cool cars; we long for these things, until one day we can afford to buy them, and then we long for something else. Or, we watch the news, and, as a result, we feel saddened or angered by all of the suffering in the world. These are just a couple of examples of how we are living merely as an effect of our surroundings. Everything we do is a reaction to something else. We go to Yale because our father went to Yale. We do what is expected of us instead of making choices.

At some point along the way, when our beautiful, romantic comedy gets shattered and becomes a horror flick, we start thinking: "Okay, what's this life about?" Often, people come to spirituality when their movie has become too painful and their whole life has been one big effect. They can't bear the chaos and suffering any-more. Kabbalah teaches us that it's time to step out of the current movie you're living and create and produce something that is entirely yours—not someone else's *Little Shop of Horrors*!

Planting Seeds

Do you ever find yourself saying: You made me angry. I can't believe *you* did this to me. *You* made me sad. As a kid, we're already learning this way of thinking in school and on the playground—this whole notion that *you* did this to me. If I'm saying *you* did this to me, then I'm saying that you're the cause and I'm the effect. I'm saying that I have no control over my reality and that life is happening *to* me. I'm disconnected from fulfillment, and I'm in a temporary state of being upset.

We need to understand that nothing happens *suddenly*. As the kabbalists tell us, Universal Law ensures that for everything that occurs or manifests in this life, something caused it. And for every tree there is a seed from which it grew. Think about it. When you look at a tree, all you see is the trunk, the branches, the leaves, and the fruit. You don't see the seed because it was concealed, but does that mean it didn't exist? Can I lift up a cup and drink from it if there was never a message from my brain telling me to do so? No, it's not possible.

The problem in life is that we misinterpret our circumstances as having no cause because we can't see the original seed. What about accidents? Accidents seem to occur randomly, but even accidents have a cause. But when we're stuck in the 1 Percent reality, we don't see how A causes B. We don't see how our selfishness or anger here caused chaos over there. We don't see the seeds that we planted.

Imagine if every time we got angry, or gossiped, or acted negatively in some way, that a hand the size of King Kong's came down out of the sky and slapped us in the head. We'd get it, wouldn't we? We'd be black and blue and bloody, but we'd know better than to say angry or selfish words again. Think of a rat in a science lab. Every time it tries to bite the cheese, it gets an electric shock. Very quickly the rat figures it out. But because we don't get slapped by an almighty hand, we start to think we got away with our negative actions. Because I was able to gossip and say nasty things about you behind your back and you weren't there to hear it, I think I'm off the hook. We have deceived ourselves, and created a huge blind spot in the process.

According to Kabbalah, one of the most negative things we can do is to cause another person humiliation. We call it "bloodshed." It's got nothing to do with shrapnel, bullets, and literal blood. It happens when we bring blood to the face, when we bring embarrassment, when we cause someone shame and humiliation. That's one of the most negative things we can do. We can't take it back once we've done it, and eventually a price will be paid.

There is a cause for every effect, but in the absence of King Kong's hand we don't usually see the effect immediately. It might take a couple of months. Or, it could lie at the seed level, beneath the surface, undetected for years and years. So as part of our excavation work, our purpose is to find the real cause of our chaos, the true cause of our conflict, and get to the root or the seed level.

The Ego

The Opponent, Satan, wants us to stay in effect mode. He doesn't want us to be the cause. If we become the cause, we connect to the 99 Percent, and Satan is out of a job. So he created the ego to keep us in effect mode, because the ego is all about self—it's all about *Me*. And *Me* is the effect. When our Opponent has us in effect mode, we are at his mercy and there is nothing we can do. The only way we can achieve change in this life is by elevating to the level of cause and cease being the effect.

In other words, the effect is the 1 Percent and the cause is the 99 Percent. The 1 Percent sends out messages that incite chaos, conflict, and selfishness. Let's call it radio station K-AOS. On the other hand, we have the radio station of the Light. Let's call it K-LIGHT. They're two very different streams of consciousness, sending out very different messages. The message that we get from the Light is to be the cause, take responsibility, take charge, share, and be active. Yes, doing this will require effort; it will require earnership.

Alternatively, the radio station that comes from the Opponent, K-AOS, will be much more attuned to what's comfortable—it's the easy listening channel. Its tunes sound something like this: *Let them change. I'm entitled. They're wrong. It's their loss. Why should I do anything for them? Why should I forgive you? Why should I share with you? Why should I open my heart to you?* This radio station encourages me to continue blaming God, other people, and the injustices in the world for my lack of fulfillment. It prompts me to wait for something good to come my way, without putting forth any effort.

One of the greatest tricks that the *Opponent* plays on us is reinforcing the notion that life is based on randomness—the idea that the world has absolutely no order to it. Kabbalists laugh at this idea. Why? Because the "Suddenly Syndrome" is simply not feasible given the laws of our Universe.

Yes, the Opponent is quite a trickster, constantly trying to convince us that he doesn't even exist. Again, the devil isn't some guy with a pitchfork. We're talking about our ego here. Our blind spot. The part of us that hides beneath the surface.

What do we say when we open our car door right into the guy next to us on a bicycle who goes flying off of his seat? "I didn't see you; you were in my blind spot." Our injured cyclist hardly sees that as a valid excuse. So, because I don't see it, it doesn't exist? This is the greatest trick the ego plays. If I don't recognize my selfishness, I'm not selfish. If I don't see the reason why I caused you pain, then there isn't one. You're just being too sensitive.

The Cancerians reading this know something about sensitivity. Someone born under the sign of Cancer has a tendency to be easily depressed, moody, or hurt. They have the hard shell of the crab, but on the inside they're soft and wounded. They avoid confrontation like the plague; that's why the crab walks sideways. How does a Cancer become the cause and not the effect of other people's insensitivity and blame? By taking the quality of sensitivity and using it to help someone else. In other words, if I'm more sensitive to how I'm affecting you, the focus is off of me and I can be much more effective in my relationships. Rather than blaming you for hurting me, I can ensure I don't hurt you. In this way we can take any potentially negative trait and turn it into something that benefits others.

One of our stumbling blocks is that we think that the ego, or our selfishness, is part of us. We think, *How can I remove my selfish-*

ness? That's part of who I am. Such a limited belief prevents us from getting in touch with who we really are. We use the ego's selfishness as a shell to protect us and to prevent others from seeing the Light that we have to offer.

Often, when people first come to Kabbalah, they worry: "If I change this one aspect of myself, it's going to change my core." But this attitude is what is stopping you from achieving your potential—everything that you think is you is just the cardboard box that holds the real gifts. We wrap ourselves in so many layers that we think the layers are who we really are. But they're not. Your selfishness, your fears, your limitations and insecurities are not you. It's only the Opponent trying to convince you that it's you! At the same time, he tries to persuade you into believing that he doesn't exist at all. Kabbalah helps us to pull back the layers and remove the mask of the Opponent.

Take the case of one new student of Kabbalah—a very shy, intro-spective, quiet kind of chap. Very English, modest, and a Pisces. He really thought he was a charming, respectful person. You know what amazed and shocked him? To discover, through Kabbalah, that his quiet introspection was actually hiding a huge ego! How, he wondered, can a shy person have an enormous ego? Surely an arrogant person, who is bragging all day long has the bigger ego. But think about it. When he was busy being shy and self-conscious, who was he obsessing about? Himself. What do you think about *me*? Do you like *me*? Are you going to laugh at *me*? When we focus on ourselves, by definition, it's our ego that's keeping us locked inside. So a shy person has to learn to let go and take risks, just as an arrogant person has to let go of trying to convince everyone that he or she is worthy of love and praise.

The Vessel

We have an immense amount of Light to share, and we share Light by removing our masks and by becoming the person we really long to be. To do this, we need an action plan. You don't go into battle without figuring out how you're going to win. If a general woke up in the morning and decided to just wing it, he'd go home defeated. In order to win, he must first organize his troops and develop a strategy. In the same manner, we need a plan in order to effectively use the tools of Kabbalah and the Light of the Creator to fight the ego and Satan. We need to prepare.

There's a funny story about a father and his son. One day, the father has a brilliant idea. He goes to a puzzle-maker and asks to buy a puzzle before it is cut up into pieces so his son can frame it and hang it on his wall, ready made. He gives the finished product to his son and the boy says: "Dad, the whole point of the puzzle is to put it together. The fun is in planning which piece goes where!" That's the work of the vessel—to develop a plan; to decide which piece goes where and what to tackle first.

First we tackle Level One of Living Kabbalah, and leave the deep stuff for later, when we feel comfortable, safe, and strong enough. There are so many issues to take on. Every single person has gone through something in their childhood—with their parents, at school, with their friends. We also battle disappointments we've faced as adults. We have lifetimes of issues to uncover. There is so much to work on that we need a plan to be able to work piece by piece, until we finish the entire puzzle.

In Kabbalah, the term *vessel* is very important. In some sense we are all vessels, and our purpose is to be filled with Light. A vessel is a container and that vessel can be limited or it can be large. Like the pieces of our puzzle, some are bigger, some smaller. We all have two eyes, one nose, one mouth, two hands, and two legs. We all have a body that's made of the same material. We all have a Soul. We all have the Light within us that we are learning to access. So what's the difference between people? Or, to put it another way, what is the difference between vessels? What determines the difference between a Donald Trump, who wants to own half a city, and a guy who is happy living in his one-bedroom apartment? Is one person better than the other? Of course not. Simply, those with a bigger desire are able to draw more to them, while those with a smaller desire are more easily satisfied.

If you're sitting in a dark room trying to read a book, it would be more efficient (and kinder to your eyes) if the light were on. But unless you actually have the desire to get up and turn on the light, that light is not going to force its way spontaneously into the room. It doesn't work that way. One of the universal principles is that the Light of fulfillment can only flow into the vessel if desire exists first. If I don't want to get married, am I going to end up walking down the aisle? If I don't want to take the corporate job, am I going to end up working in a corporation? Again, there is no coercion. We first have to create our vessel by having desire.

A bigger vessel, by the way, doesn't mean more fulfillment. Remember, the bigger the pot, the bigger the lid you need to put on top. The greater the need or desire to receive, the greater the need to restrict potential greediness. Think of a person who is an overnight success and receives a great deal of attention. Everyone adores him, and he becomes a primadonna. He went from nothing to everything. What can we say about this person? He has an enormous ego, but it doesn't necessarily mean he has enormous fulfillment. It's important to understand that the greater the ego, the greater the blockage. Yes, the greater vessel has potential to draw more Light, but we have to be more capable of managing that energy.

To become the cause, we need to know that we're making a choice. Once we're making a choice, we can take responsibility. Once we're making a choice, nothing happens *to* me; it happens *by* me. But often we don't even know we're making choices. The most important lesson that we can take from this chapter is that *we have a choice.* From now on, our lives can be different, if that is what we desire. Things that have gotten us into trouble before can lead us to happiness today.

Cause vs. Effect

All it takes is a switch in perception: *I choose to be the cause, not the effect. I choose to be a strong vessel; I choose to be the Light.* If we choose to remain an effect, our life will continue to be a mess. When we live our life in the 1 Percent, the effect will be chaos—guaranteed. What we get in return is the comfort of knowing what tomorrow will be like. Becoming the cause by tapping into the 99 Percent and stepping out of being an effect will take some getting used to. That's because when we start moving into cause mode, closer to the Light, we're stepping into unknown territory. Yes, we feel more real. Yes, it feels better. Yes, it feels more fulfilling, but it starts bringing up some uncomfortable stuff.

I went with my wife and a group of friends to see the band Coldplay performing. My wife was at the beginning of her pregnancy. The band started playing and I was enjoying it. Somewhere, toward the middle of the concert, I realized that my wife was having a tough time. Then I started to cry. I saw that she was there to support my desire unconditionally without thinking of herself. And it got me thinking: *What in my life is like that? What in my life is unconditional? What in my life is really important? What if you had no one in your life at this moment that supported you unconditionally?*

As Coldplay was playing, I thought how my wife, my kids, my mom and dad are all in my life unconditionally. Then I started thinking: *Who belongs in my life? Who doesn't? Who do I need to work with to make our relationship better? Who is taking from me? Who am I taking from?* In that one moment, all of my relationships became clear. It was like a total reboot. When your computer goes down, you reboot it. It's not a big deal. In life, we don't think we have that same choice. We do.

[Light-Work]

Take a blank piece of paper and write the name of every single significant person in your life. Then ask yourself this: Do they belong in my life? If yes, why? If they don't belong, then why are they there? Is it time to have a conversation with them? Is it time to remove them from your movie? Start re-thinking and re-choosing the people you have around you.

Doing this was an amazing experience for me—one that I've inserted into my life in a regular way. I think about this often, and believe that we all need to do this. The question becomes more than just, where am I going? But just as importantly, who is going with me?

If your life is like a boat, who do you want in your boat with you? You want people that support you. People that help you be the cause. People that help you live in the 99 Percent. People who drive you nuts don't belong there unless they are prompting you to change an aspect of your nature. And we don't belong in someone else's life if all we're doing is draining their energy. It's time to get real and be the cause of the one who comes with us along our journey.

Chapter 6
Being the Cause

Hopefully, by now you're noticing some significant shifts beginning to occur in your understanding of yourself and your life, and how the Universe operates. That's what Kabbalah is all about: perspective.

Did you think about all the people in your life who have significance for you? Are they there because you've chosen them? Are you blaming them for the conflicts you feel they're causing you? Or are you choosing them with appreciation and recognizing the gifts they bring to you?

In Kabbalah, we don't just choose what we like and ignore what we don't like. Instead, we ask these questions: *Why is this in my movie? Why is this person upsetting me? Why is this person bringing me love and happiness? How did I merit such a wonderful experience or such terrible hardships?* Of course, the ego wants to take credit for all of the good and reject the bad. But we have chosen every aspect of our reality, for better or worse.

Blame

When we're not choosing, when we're acting like the effect. We call that "victim consciousness." This consciousness says: *I don't claim responsibility for anything; I don't recognize the real cause; If you get me upset and I'm experiencing something I don't want to feel, I'll make you responsible for it.* Thoughts like these can be very influential, but they have no basis in truth, according to Kabbalah.

"Why is it that our parents push our buttons the most?" Well, they're the ones that were there when we installed them; they know exactly where they are. This makes it easy to blame our parents and use that as the reason as to why we're in a pattern that never changes. We can fill our mind with excuses: *I wasn't loved; My father abandoned me; I don't deserve love; I am entitled.* There's no end to the reasons we can create for why our life is a certain way.

After all, we are the authors of our life. We write the script, so if our movie is not using the script we want, it is up to us to edit it. A powerful example of this is Victor Frankel, the famous psychoanalyst and philosopher, who was also a Holocaust survivor. Many of his written works reflected that, although he saw tremendous destruction, death, and horror—lost his entire family and had every reason to feel like a victim—in his consciousness, he continued to see the bigger picture in order to grow from what he experienced.

Another example of a person who had a choice of remaining a victim or becoming the cause was Christopher Reeve. When he fell off a horse and became paralyzed, at first he wanted to die. He begged his wife Dana to pull the plug on his life support. She insisted that he give her thirty days and if he felt the same way after the thirty days, she would pull the plug. Thirty days later, he decided he wanted to fight. For the next nine years, he accomplished things that his doctor said were medically impossible. And he inspired millions of people with his courage. Now, instead of remembering him as the character of Superman, we remember him as a life-changer, a person who had a choice and chose not be a victim, but to do more for the world, for himself, and for his family.

We must constantly ask ourselves, are we reacting as a victim or acting as the cause? It's one or the other. If we're in effect mode, then the world happens to us. There will always be someone—the doctor, the lawyer, the garbage man—who we can designate as the cause of our misery. Or we can choose to be the cause and look at what we can do to effect change.

There are no accidents

Nothing randomly falls out of the sky and into our lives. Every effect has a cause. In that way, coincidences don't really exist. When we talk about synchronicity, when everything seems to line up just right, it's because we've created a condition that brings those pieces together. Synchronicity occurs by design. The family you were born into was not a mistake; you didn't pick the wrong parents. The circumstances that you found yourself in as a child were not meant to be someone else's circumstances. We learn, in Kabbalah, that what belongs to us will come to us. And what is not ours will never stay with us. We have exactly the circumstances in front of us that we need.

As I said before, there is no coercion in spirituality. Universal Law dictates that the Creator cannot force you into a situation you can't handle. When you're in a situation that feels overwhelming, remember, it's a trick of the ego. The ego might convincingly say: *I'm not able to handle this one. I think I'll pass.* But if it's in front of you, the Creator knows you are ready to handle it. We deceive ourselves when we tell ourselves we're not ready, we can't take responsibility, we are a victim, or we can't handle it.

How are we going to grow unless we face difficult challenges?

When you go to a gym, how do you build muscle? By using resistance—a force that works against a weight, allowing us to build muscle mass. There is no way in life that we can create greatness or expand our vessel unless we have something to resist or work against. That's why the Opponent exists. When we're in the game of life, we need opposition against which we can play. Otherwise we won't feel fulfilled.

Leaving Behind Victimhood

How do we go from being a victim to being the cause? Imagine for a moment growing up with a very critical parent, an abusive father. On the one hand, as a grownup, we have a choice: We can blame our father for our circumstances. We can even take on those abusive qualities and act out in the same way, generation after generation. Or we can stop and say: *Wait a minute. You know what? In some respects, I need to thank the Creator and even thank my father for the awful things he taught me as a parent. I have been shown exactly how not to treat my child. I see that if I want to continue to be a victim, I can simply act negatively, selfishly, abusively, and propel the same kind of chaos into the next generation. Or I can recognize that behaviors such as my father's failure to create trust, faith, certainty, love, and connection. Now, I know exactly how to foster more closeness, respect, and self-esteem in my child. I can completely transform my experience and bring something positive to my own family.*

I learned a very valuable lesson firsthand. Some time ago, my father suffered a stroke. After that, I saw him less often. We used to study Kabbalah together at three A.M., having conversations that lasted for hours. I used to spend at least ten to twenty hours a week with him. When the stroke happened, I felt as though the Creator caused my father to have a massive stroke and that a part of my father had died for me. *Why did the Universe do this?* I thought. Eventually, I saw that I had been looking at him as if he was less of a person instead of trying to connect with him on a different level. Instead of connecting more, I had been connecting less.

I realized that I had been feeling like a victim, and I started to cry. We lose so much when we feel like a victim. That moment was a turning point. Since then, I have been working on really being there with my father. It's difficult, but it's something that we're doing together. And as a result of going through my father's painful and scary experience with him, I'm becoming more open about my own personal story, more willing to expose my own inner process. I am growing from this challenging circumstance.

One of the Centre's teachers talks about a time when he was eleven years old and was sent to boarding school. It wasn't his decision, but as much as he argued, complained, cried, wrote hate mail to his parents, and threatened to run away, the situation didn't change. For years afterwards, he blamed the fact that he was sent to boarding school for all of his problems, his shutting down emotionally, for becoming cold, distant, and mistrustful of people. The fact is that many aspects of boarding school helped him to grow up, be independent, and become self-sufficient. He learned to be a man and take care of himself. But he used that victim consciousness to shut down emotionally in his marriage twenty years later.

How can we tell when we're still playing the victim, or if we've moved out of that mode into being the cause? One obvious clue is checking to see if those negative, self-defeating patterns are still around. If we're still complaining about how unhappy we are, how defeated we are, how nobody loves us, how there are no good women in L.A., or how there are no good men in New York, then we have not broken the pattern. We have not changed anything. The script is the same. We're complaining about being in the same boring movie that we're creating!

Another clue that you're in the old effect mode instead of cause mode is if you are trying to change your self using the 1 Percent, like getting a new car or going on a shopping spree because you want to feel better about yourself. That's not being the cause: it's being an effect. You're still trying to derive happiness from the outside world instead of creating it from within.

There is an interesting story about a kabbalist who, before he goes to sleep at night, asks the Creator: "Please, show me a glimpse of heaven. I want to see what it is we're all striving for. If our Soul leaves this world, where does it go?" So his Soul ascends and is met by an angel, who says: "Come, let's go for a ride." The kabbalist goes with the angel along this path. They're going and going. Finally, they see two people sitting on a battered bench, with a cracked glass of water and stale bread that looks like it's been there for three months.

The kabbalist asks the angel: "What is this?"

"This is heaven."

"What do you mean this is heaven? How could this be heaven?"

One of the men on the bench looks at him and says: "You don't understand, heaven is not somewhere you go—it's not a destination—heaven is within you. We're the best of friends and we love each other, despite the cracked glass, the stale bread, and the chipped wood. This, my friend, *is* Heaven."

As long as we view heaven or happiness as a place or destination, we will remain in effect mode and will never see the heaven that is already with us. We're sure to feel deprived of joy, like a victim. But when we find the strength to look within for our happiness, then we become the cause.

You can tell if you're really getting to the root cause of your chaos by using this simple analogy: we all know that weeds can become destructive forces that can take over our beautiful garden. So, how do we combat this? We pull up the weeds. We remove the problem. But we all know that, unless we get to the roots of those weeds, they will inevitably come back. In much the same way, we have to dig down to the roots of our discontent if we are to rid ourselves of its devastating effects.

If a brunette is trying to dye her hair blonde, every few weeks she'll have to deal with the roots that have become brown again. To make someone permanently blonde who was once brunette, we'd have to change her DNA to get to the root, so to speak, of the problem. We begin to change our spiritual DNA when we commit to doing the necessary work to transform our patterns.

What does this mean for me and my relationships? If the core issue for me in a relationship is a fear of abandonment, the fear that everyone I meet is going to leave me, and I never address this fear, I am only reinforcing the pattern. If I approach my partner from the standpoint of: "You don't love me; you're going to leave me," and my partner is constantly having to reassure me by saying: "No, I love you. Of course I'm here for you," then this pattern will become old in a hurry. My partner will grow tired and will end the relationship, and I will be left saying: "Well, I knew you were going to leave me in the first place." But, who is really doing the leaving here? Who is causing it? I suggest that it is the person with the fear and insecurity, who never learned to develop trust. If we don't get to our core fears and belief systems, the destructive blind spots that we've talked about, we will never experience different results. We'll be living the same movie over and over again, only with different characters.

Not only do we run the risk of falling into the victim mentality, but also others will try to suck us into their victim movie. Scorpios, for example, can be professional victims who try to pull us into their movie by convincing us that we caused their suffering. It's in their DNA. Again, every sign has pros and cons. That's their con. They can be professional victims and they suck us in. They try to put the blame on us. We need to be strong not only so we don't fall into victimhood, but also so that others don't drag us into their victim consciousness. What we really need are the tools of Kabbalah.

[Exercise]

I want to take this opportunity to introduce another k-Tool; it's a question that I want you to think about: *What am I sowing today that I will reap ten years from now? Am I creating fulfillment or chaos? Am I sowing weeds or am I sowing beautiful flowers?*

Close your eyes. Sit quietly and go back in your mind to a time when you felt like you were a victim. See yourself in the situation. Recognize how painful it was. How angry you felt. How hurt, betrayed, ripped off, and abandoned it made you feel. Chances are that this is something that didn't go away quickly; it's burned into your memory. Maybe you don't have to go back too far in time; this situation might be happening to you right now. We all have a list of resentments that we can recall at any time. That's how vivid and present these experiences are in our minds.

Recall how you felt. Notice your attitude. Notice how defensive you've become. How did this happen to me? Why me? Notice how paralyzed, how stuck you feel. Are you still stuck in this self-defeating pattern? Now ask yourself this question: *What will happen if I stay in this place of blaming?*

What will happen in your next relationship? How will you deal with the next challenging boss? The next challenging customer who is complaining? How will you handle your kids when they start testing you? It's difficult to see clearly when you're in the thick of your chaos. When we're in the throes of our blaming and complaining, we don't recognize how our ego takes over and causes us to judge, to complain, and to become a victim. That's one of the most difficult things about transformation: we don't see our own blind spots. But by using visualization and completing our written work, we can help bring them to light.

[Light-Work]

Identify a relationship in which you were the effect. Maybe it was with your boss, with your parents growing up, your spouse, or maybe it's happening now with your child or a friend. Choose a relationship in which you're a victim. *How do you feel?*

Are these the kinds of feelings you want? If you don't challenge these feelings, interpretations, judgments, or conclusions you're drawing, will the results of the next relationship, scenario, or challenge in your life be any different? Is this place where you feel empowered where you want to be?

What is your choice? You can either be the cause or remain the effect.

Let's turn this scenario around. How can you go from blaming to creating a different situation? Remember, the first step is to stop, to pause: *Wait a minute, what's going on here? How did I get into this situation? Why is this in my movie, and what can I do to transform it?* That's what I would like you to do—explore a relationship or scenario in which you are the effect and evoke all the feelings you have about it.

There is a payoff to being the effect—you don't have to take any responsibility. You get to be passive. But the downside is that nothing will ever change, and you will never experience the type of fulfillment you are seeking. Right now you have an opportunity to identify what you need to do differently. If you don't, this scenario will repeat itself over and over again unless you, and only you, correct it at the seed level. That's the law of cause and effect. You have a choice as to whether you will be the cause of new results or the effect of the same pattern. Make the choice to be the cause in your life, and see just how amazing your life will be a year from now!

Ego &
Opponent

Chapter 7
Ego & Opponent

In the last chapter's Light-Work, we considered the questions: *What if I never change? What if I continue to be the effect in all the areas of my life?* What were your conclusions? We're going to build from those conclusions in this next chapter. So far, we've been talking about the big picture, fundamental laws of the Universe: the idea that we are the creators of our own reality, and what happens when we don't take on that role in our life. Now we're going to focus on why it's so difficult to do that.

What is it that keeps us stuck and prevents us from truly being the cause of everything in our life? What does it mean to be stuck? Why does chaos stay with us even though we're smart, well-meaning, and have good intentions? How come we continue to stay in the same negative, unsatisfying, and sometimes painful relationships? Remember, we're doing some excavation here. It's important to stay open to the adventure. Don't allow the Opponent to shut you down as we go through this process. If there is true Light to be revealed, the Opponent will always do his best to take that Light from us.

A good indicator that our excavation work is paying off is that we will start to feel challenged; we will start to feel resistance. Parts of us will want to shut down. I've noticed during classes and workshops that when we start to talk about the Opponent, about our reactive nature, about the part of us that can shut down and act out, students start checking out. They get uncomfortable, stop paying attention, and begin doodling. At that point, I always remind students to note the resistance that comes up, because this is an indication that the Opponent in us has been triggered.

There is a game going on here. There is a battle between Light and darkness. We're after the Light from the Creator. We're after fulfillment. So is our ego. The difference is that the ego wants you to settle for short-term gains. The Light is in it for the long haul.

The Opponent

The Opponent is not an enemy outside of us; it's within us. The ego wants to take away your Light in order to strengthen itself. It's a bit like telling someone who is already arrogant how amazing and fabulous he is—we're only helping to strengthen that person's ego. We're feeding more energy to the Opponent. In the same way, when we begin to transform ourselves and move from being the effect to being the cause, the Opponent becomes alerted. His warning bells go off, saying: *Wait a minute! Be careful. I*

*sense a desire to change in someone. Better get in there and
stomp it out fast.*

Pay attention to any resistance you feel. Are you zoning out? Do
you want to stop reading or not do the Light-Work? These are
easy feelings. You're only a threat to the Opponent if you're starting to transform your nature.

We have two choices in life: we can be the cause and have Light
and fulfillment, or we can descend into ego consciousness and
wind up with destruction and chaos. It's one or the other. There is
no in-between. In this world, most people are living in some form
of chaos. Even if they have everything, there is still chaos,
because most people are not working on removing their ego.

Even when we know something is good for us, it's sometimes
hard to follow through. I'm challenged with food and sugar. I'm
constantly on a diet or working out because my metabolism is not
fast enough to burn off the extra calories. I lose thirty or forty
pounds; then I gain it back. I sign up for the gym, go twice, and
"forget" to go back. Knowing what is good for me and actually
doing it are two separate things.

Some of the smartest people make the stupidest mistakes. A
Harvard grad, top of his class, ends up in chaos from a stupid
ethical mistake. Why? Because it's not about intelligence; it's
about ego. When ego is left unchecked, it will pick the worst scenario out of a hundred, out of a thousand. That's how ego operates. Ego equals chaos. Ego equals the worst possible outcomes. If there is one person in this world that will be the most

difficult for you to deal with and will cause you the most suffering, that's the one with whom you'll end up. They may look good. They may lure you in, but, in the end, they're going to cause you pain.

A lot of people have been to therapy or done some self-help work and think that the ego has a healthy component. They think ego means self-esteem or self-worth. According to Kabbalah, there is no positive aspect of ego; there is no positive aspect of a blockage. Someone with self-esteem, who wants to be successful, has a healthy desire, according to Kabbalah. It has nothing to do with ego.

But remember, you can have the Desire to Receive for the Self Alone—selfish desire, which *is* the ego—or you can have a big desire to accomplish more, be more, and share more. So when we use the term *ego* in Kabbalah, we're not talking about something good. There are no positive attributes of ego. The only purpose of the ego is to keep us mired in our own garbage.

Different Aspects of Ego

Often people who appear overly confident are only covering up their low self-worth with an egotistical exterior. So not only are they overlooking the real problem of low self-esteem, they are also burying it under a shell of ego. The ego does two things: 1) It protects us from our hidden lack of desire and self-worth, and 2) It distracts us from the real problem. In other words, the ego is killing us twice.

My father, the Rav, gives a beautiful description of humility. What does it mean to be humble? According to the Rav, it means always recognizing our need to ask for help. It's a very simple thing. Those who suffer from low self-esteem and insecurity tend to overcompensate. They may act as if they know everything. But if we already know everything, how can we receive more? If we claim to know everything about ourselves, what are we saying? That we don't have any blind spots? There is nothing else for us to learn?

We don't see ourselves the way other people see us. We have no idea how selfish we can be. Guaranteed, there are people in this world who see things about us that are obvious, yet, when we look at ourselves, we don't see the same things. These are our blind spots—blockages or areas of behavior that are obvious to others but not to us. It's not like the car driving alongside that we can't see in the side view mirror, but more like the car right in front of us that we can't see because we're blinded by the glare of ego. And not seeing our blind spots gets us into real trouble—just like when we don't see the Mack truck bearing down on us!

We also know that people are usually not willing to hear about their blind spots if we try to tell them what we see. You can't convince a friend that their choice in a potential spouse is not a good one. Or take, for example, those who are addicted, acting out with alcohol, drugs, gambling, or whatever it is. We can see how much pain they're in, but trying to get them to see the destruction they are causing is another issue entirely. They'll act as if it's not really a problem. The denial of the ego is unbelievable.

A classic example is a woman who is being abused by her husband. She remains in the relationship because, in her distorted way of understanding, she sees the abuse as a form of love and attention. In other words, she'd rather get beaten than risk the discomfort of having to become independent and be the cause of her reality. It's sad and brutal, but the equation has two sides: the ego of the abuser and, just as powerful, the ego of the person being abused because she's blind to her role in it.

There's a big difference between pain and suffering. Sometimes we go through painful situations. We go through loss. We go through tremendous challenges that can be truly unpleasant. But kabbalists have an unusual view of suffering. What is suffering? Suffering is choosing to hold onto pain and not allowing it to pass. This is the root of chaos.

And the ego is addicted to chaos. Chaos does not refer only to abuse, addiction, or extreme situations. You walk into Starbucks thinking of that grande mocha latte that you intend to buy, but you've forgotten your wallet at home. You become frustrated. That's chaos. You walk down the street and stub your toe. Ouch! That's chaos. We experience moments of chaos every day. If we continue down this path, we'll eventually end up in extreme situations. But before that, our day could be filled with ten, twenty, thirty occasions where we feel a little pain because of external circumstances.

We don't think of shyness as ego. We don't think of insecurity and being self-conscious and introspective as ego. But whether we're arrogant, puffed up, and constantly boasting, or we're cowering in the corner afraid and insecure about exposing ourselves to others, the focus of our attention is the same in both instances. What are we focused on? Ourselves. It's always a shock to realize that those of us who are shy are usually obsessed with other people's opinions. We've become self-absorbed in our fear: *What do they think of me? I will never be good enough. I'll never be able to compete. I can never compare to that person.* So we shrink away and become the effect of our fear. Ultimately, it's still ego.

Fear, anger, competitiveness, insecurity, low self-esteem, selfishness, envy, anxiety, impatience—they all have their root in ego. Personally, I'm scared of heights. My brother took me parasailing in Mexico. When it was my turn, I began hyperventilating and couldn't do it. Even my fear of parasailing goes back to ego, because fear is the ego's language. It keeps us from growing and trying new things.

Instant Gratification

There is another aspect of ego, which is our drive for instant gratification. Fearful, and searching for comfort, we want a quick fix. We want to get that selfish rush of excitement and energy. We don't want to take the time to go through a process. We want it now! Why do you think so many of us struggle with sugar, alcohol, and stimulants like caffeine? Because we want the energy at once, even though it means we'll need three or four cups of coffee to sustain the energy, or have to keep eating sugar to get it.

We're happy to do it in the moment. Later, we regret the gained weight and the sense of being uncomfortable in our own bloated bodies. But at the critical moment we choose instant gratification. When you think about it, it's ridiculous. How many of us complain about our weight? If you look at someone who is content—happy with their physical body and their lifestyle—they eat basically healthy foods. They don't have that need for instant gratification. They're happy to eat broccoli. They're happy to stay off of wheat, sugar, dairy, and alcohol. They don't complain about it. They're in control of what's going on; their desires don't control them. There is no guilt or shame, just effort and discipline, which offers a huge payoff in the form of satisfaction.

Ego is Us

How then do we plug into the Light? How do we reveal joy and happiness in our life? How do we tap into that boundless energy? Only through transforming our nature. The ego will keep us from doing it. It will keep us stuck. In fact, the energy we could be tapping into goes to support the ego and only serves to thicken its armor. Our ego prevents us from having discipline. It promotes laziness, comfort, and lack of accountability. The ego doesn't want to budge. That's why we become so stubborn. We don't want to change. And that is the influence of the Opponent, the ego.

The ego isn't us. We may be afraid to lose it, but it's not us. It was never us. It didn't come into the world with us and it's not going to leave with us. It's a suit we put on. No matter how many layers of ego you have on, it's never going to be part of you. The code word for ego in kabbalistic wisdom is the Desire to Receive for the Self Alone. We are the only ones ego considers. We may think that we're going to use the ego to take care of others, but it's not true. Ego considers only us.

Your friend says, "The Brooklyn Bridge is for sale; I'll sell it to you." But you'd be crazy to fall for this offer. The Brooklyn Bridge belongs to the country. It belongs to the world. Yet every single day the ego tries to sell us the Brooklyn Bridge and we buy it. Not only do we buy it, but we overpay. And we think we got a steal! We think that it's the best thing for us and that it's cheaper than taking a risk. The truth is, every single day we fall for what we think is a bargain and we pay dearly for it. Our payment is not money. Our payment is chaos.

Five Extensions of Ego

Every day the ego is selling us something new. One day, all your problems are everyone else's fault. The next day you beat your-self up because you're a loser. The ego keeps morphing. It's a multiple personality, with many changes of clothing, many faces, and even many different names. The devil, Lucifer, the Dark Side, the monster in the closet: all of these names suggest that the ego is something "out there."

One of the greatest Kabbalists, Rav Isaac Luria, explains that there are five extensions of the ego: anger, hatred, judgment, control, and pride. These are the branches of the tree of ego—the ways our ego can manifest. We all have the capacity to get upset. We all judge. We are all obsessed with trying to have some degree of control. We all tend to be self-important sometimes; this is pride. We get angry at people. We don't think of ourselves as having hatred, but it's amazing the thoughts we have when we get into a debate with people over war and politics. Ego can reach into all corners of our life, when we allow it. As long as we are blocked, with the ego controlling our thoughts, feelings, and actions, we can never become the cause of our own fulfillment.

You might want to think about these five extensions of the ego. Consider the following: *Where in my life do I have aspects of anger, judgment, hatred, control, or pride? Where do I have a sense of being self-important? Where is it hard for me to let someone in, or hard for me to let someone know that I don't have my act together? When do I feel embarrassed? That's pride talking. Do I try to manipulate people to like me and approve of me? That's control. Do I wish that I had what someone else has? Do I feel inadequate or compare myself with others? This is judgment turned inward.*

Our first reaction to something is usually ego-inspired. A situation comes up, and bang! We have an immediate reaction—that's ego. The secondary reaction is usually inspired by the Light. But if we don't act on this secondary impulse, then the ego takes over. We have a five-to-ten-second window after the first reaction to figure it out: *Okay, maybe I'm not going to do that. What am I going to do instead?* Then the secondary voice comes in. But, if we don't listen to that soft voice, we're done. We usually have only a very small window of time in which to defeat the ego.

Embarrassment & Crushing the Ego

How many times does someone say something about our personality that embarrasses us? When someone tells us we're acting selfishly, were being controlling, or that we've hurt that person's feelings, our initial response is to get defensive. We feel insulted. But if we waited five or ten seconds before reacting, we might realize that that person is right. *Maybe I am selfish and I've just been busted. I've been confronted about my selfishness, and I don't want to look at it. Now, I feel embarrassed.* According to Kabbalah, this is a great thing. The more we can take a moment to consider the ego, the more we have a chance of taking control of its energy. But after briefly considering that this person might be right, we usually disregard that notion and go back to our movie instead: *I will crush that person who embarrassed me.*

So we have these two radio stations constantly bombarding us. The ego is playing loud music, so loud that sometimes we can't hear the faint melodic music on the other station. Which one are you going to listen to? The loud one, of course, the one screaming for your attention. If a car drives by blasting loud music, you can't help but listen to it. You forget about the soft music that is playing on your own radio. The ego is loud; it screams. But it's not real; there is nothing underneath to support it. The soft music has the support of the Light.

When someone hurts us or embarrasses us, our immediate reaction is to shout or embarrass them back. Our secondary reaction is to consider that they might be right. If we don't stop there and listen to that quiet voice, we get sucked right back into the ego.

[Light-Work]

One of the two major principles we've discussed in this chapter is how we allow our ego to take control of our actions, despite recognizing the negative consequences. I want you to look back at your actions today. When did you act out of ego? Did you come from a place of anger, hatred, pride, judgment, or control? Make a list.

The other major principle that we discussed is the existence of two distinct voices that compete for our attention, the two radio stations we can listen to: the Opponent's voice, or the quiet, concealed voice of the Light. Did you hear the voice of the Light today? What was it saying to you?

If you feel like you have a grasp of what we've talking about and you're in touch with what it is you did and which voice you listened to, take it one step further. Ask two or three of your friends what you really need to work on. Be very specific about who you ask. They should be people who really care about you, know you well, and people who you respect. People you trust will tell you the truth. Ask them: *What is it you see in me that's negative or destructive?* It's important to listen. Your friends, if they recognize that you trust them and are sincere in your desire to know the truth, will tell you. Your ego will be a little insulted, which is good. In fact, it's a wonderful gift. See if you can take in the wisdom that someone is giving you, because we simply cannot see our own blind spots.

The other way you might shed light on your ego is by asking your-self this: *When was I lazy today? Did I tend to procrastinate or avoid doing something? Have I been withholding from someone? Did I avoid dealing with a confrontation or conflict I needed to address?* Remember, these are other ways in which the ego can show up in our lives.

Enter all these thoughts in your journal. In this way, you are begin-ning to remove ego and all if its destructive defense mechanisms from your life. You're starting to dig into the anger, to get under-neath the control, to deflate the pride. Stay on track by remaining open and willing to uncover all of the guises of the ego.

Chapter 8
Crushing the Ego

Look back at your Light-Work from the previous chapter and remember the five extensions of the ego: anger, judgment, control, hatred, and pride. The ego can take control of us in many different ways. Have you been paying attention to when the voice of the ego starts to interfere? What kind of messages are you getting? Did you ask a trusted friend what you need to look at in yourself? Did you react to what he or she told you? Once we are willing to be humble and ask for help, in that moment we have a chance to take control over our ego.

Please know that you're not alone in doing this work. Every one of us who studies Kabbalah is doing this Light-Work. This is part of what we do, and I'm no exception.

Crushing the Ego

Now that we've identified the ego as our Opponent, now we get to destroy it! I call it "crushing the ego." Bring to mind an image of a nut, something with a tough shell like a Brazil nut. It takes a tremendous amount of force to break that shell. The greater the resistance and strength of the ego, the greater the force needed to crush it. Someone who has been employing a powerful defense mechanism might need to be pummeled by life in order to penetrate to the real core of who that person is.

If we want to produce a diamond—the real nature of Light within us—how much pressure do we need to put on the coal? We've all gone through pain in life, including disappointment and failure. Underneath it lies a diamond. Our commitment now is to that diamond—the path that leads us to the most fulfillment. If you leave a chunk of coal on the table, it's never going to become a priceless gem. Even if you put a pound of pressure on the coal, you will never produce a diamond. You need tremendous force over a long period of time! That's what we are doing here—putting crushing pressure on the ego.

I often use the analogy of a steam room when discussing how to handle the pressure of difficult circumstances. If you sit in a steam room or sauna, there's an amazing sense of release and relaxation as you enjoy the heat and start sweating. Maybe there's menthol eucalyptus in the air, and it smells great. Then the jets turn on or water splashes on the hot coals, and it gets really, really hot. You're barely tolerating the heat. Even though you're experiencing something very healthy, you start to feel uncomfortable.

Then comes the moment when you bolt for the door, because you can't take the heat anymore; you're just too uncomfortable.

How do you learn to endure the discomfort associated with breaking the ego or the tendency to become defensive or feel insulted? It's a bit like allowing yourself to stay another minute or two in the steam room in order to build up a tolerance. *Okay, I'll take the heat for another minute. Maybe next time I'll be able to tolerate an extra two minutes.*

Our ego has us believe that we should avoid at all costs any possibility of being hurt, any chance of being disappointed, or any likelihood that we might be insulted. The paradox is that the more humiliated we are, the more embarrassed we become, and the more uncomfortable we feel, the more helpful it is for breaking the ego. If we allow ourselves to be uncomfortable in public, we improve our chances of building our core strength. In fact, when someone embarrasses us in public, according to Kabbalah, it causes a tremendous crushing of the ego.

Who am I?

After all, who is it that gets embarrassed? Is it us, our core, or is the clothing, the ego? It's the ego. Who are we? Not what we wear; that's not us. We're underneath that. We are not our heart, because a person could receive a new heart, someone else's heart, and still be himself. We are not our arms and legs, nor our brain. A person could have a stroke and rehabilitate the body and the mind. Our core exists on a higher level, the Soul level. That Soul level is truly who we are.

Who we are at the core doesn't get embarrassed, doesn't feel good when somebody else gets hurt, doesn't feel validated when we've gotten our way, and doesn't feel better when we feel like a victim. These external forces don't make or break our core being. Our 99 Percent, our core, doesn't feel bad when the ego fails or gets embarrassed. On the contrary, we get pushed to the next higher level when we go through embarrassment, because we're removing more of the ego.

We're so accustomed to protecting and guarding ourselves that we come up with all sorts of ways to overcompensate for insecurity. We try to look good. We try to be slick. We try to look like we have all the answers. We try to be "Yes" men and women to gain approval and to please others, because we're so terrified that, if we're rejected, we won't be loved anymore. You know what? We do get rejected, and there are people who have stopped loving us. But those experiences are opportunities in disguise.

Let's say the Creator is trying to bring us our soul mate, but we're in a lousy relationship that we're holding onto for all the wrong reasons—we admire this other person, but we can't have a conversation with him or her; there's no emotional connection. If we allow ourselves to admit it, we know that we're not as compatible as we thought. The Creator is trying to say to us: "Hey, your soul mate is around the corner, but he can't arrive if you don't get out of this relationship." But the ego becomes stubborn. We hold on. We like the attention we get with this attractive person on our arm.

We're afraid to end the relationship because of what others will think. People will judge us, we think. But there will always be people who will judge us. The ego is obsessed with making sure that people don't judge us, but it's an exercise in futility. People will have their opinions no matter what, and we have to allow them to do just that. The bottom line is that their opinions are none of our business. What a relief that is!

Embarrassment

There's a story about a kabbalist who comes to a town in Russia, and he can sense the presence of the Light, the taste of the Garden of Eden. He follows the trail, knowing there is something very powerful here. Like a car with a GPS, he knows where to make a left and where to make a right. Finally, he comes to a house and knocks on the door. He says to the old man who answers: "Could you let me in? There is something very special in this house."

The old man doesn't know about Kabbalah; he doesn't know who this person is, but he opens the door and lets the kabbalist in. The kabbalist walks upstairs to the bedroom and opens a closet where he finds a clown suit hanging. The kabbalist says, "Please, can you tell me the story of this suit?"

The old man is a little embarrassed, but he says: "Okay, I'll tell you the story. My father—who has passed away—his job was to collect money and give it to the needy, the homeless, the poor, the starving. One day, after he finished his work, he went into a pub for a drink. A man walked over to him, practically in tears, and said: 'Could you help me? I owe 500 rubles to the government and if I don't pay it back by tonight, they will take my daughter as a slave.'

"My father said, 'I've finished my work for the day. I've asked everyone I usually go to and they've already given me money. There's really nothing I can do.'

"The distraught man pleaded with him, 'Please, please, please, you are my last hope. I've gone to everyone I know. I've done everything, and I'm sure you can help me.' Then my father remembered there was one person in town that he hadn't asked for money in many, many months. He said, 'There is a person who usually gives nothing; he doesn't like to share. However, for you, I am going to ask him.'

"He knocked on the door of this selfish person, who greeted him with: 'What do you want? Why are you waking me up in the middle of the night?'

"My father said, 'I have a strange request. There is a person, whose daughter is about to be taken as a slave. Could you lend him 500 rubles?' The man was about to slam the door in his face when my father said, 'Wait! Ask me to do anything, anything at all, anything you want. Isn't there something I could do for you to give me this money?'

"The man said, 'Actually, I am in the mood for some entertainment. I have a clown suit. If you put it on and walk around, make people laugh, and embarrass yourself, I've give you the 500 rubles.'

"It was around 11 at night and no one was around. So my father thought, 'I'll put the clown suit on and run through town. No one is going to know.' He made the deal, put on the clown suit, and started walking into town. He didn't really want anyone to see him. Meanwhile, the man, who had come along to have fun, was making noise and waking everyone up. He kept hollering, 'Hey, look at this fool!' People started throwing rocks and eggs and vegetables at my father, the fool walking around in the middle of the night in a clown suit.

"My father was so terribly embarrassed, but he remembered that his actions were saving a girl from being a slave. So he took the pain. It wasn't the physical pain of the eggs and the tomatoes or even the rocks. It was the humiliation that really hurt, but he knew that the girl was more important than his ego.

"The kabbalist then said, 'This clown suit is the most important piece of clothing that your father ever wore! That day, your father forgot about his ego to such an extent that he connected purely to the Light.' The kabbalist asked to be buried in that clown suit instead of the usual burial garments, because he knew that this suit contained the power of the Light, pure Light, with all darkness and selfishness removed. When the kabbalist was buried in that clown suit, his Soul went straight to heaven."

Who gets embarrassed?

The first lesson in trying to understand the ego, in trying to crush the ego, is to remember that the ego is separate from us. What gets hurts when we're humiliated, what is pained, what gets affected, is only a piece of clothing, something external. It's not our essence.

I was watching Chris Rock on HBO, and he said something that struck me. He said there are three people inside us. The first person is who we really are. The second person is who we want to be. And the third is who we want everyone else to think we are. I was thinking to myself, *wow!* Most of us invest our time in that person we are selling to everybody else, who we want to be perceived as. That's person number one. Sometimes, we'll even invest time in who we want to be, but almost never do we invest in who we are.

Ego is all about who we want to be and who we want to sell ourselves as. A life without ego means we are who we are, and what we show on the outside is the same as what resides on the inside—our inner essence is displayed to everyone. Whoever we try to sell ourselves as could never be as powerful, or as fulfilling, as who we really are.

Vulnerability

We are so governed by other people's judgments and opinions of us and our ego's desire to look good in their eyes, that it takes great strength to show our weaknesses to the world, to show our vulnerability. When a person is displaying control or anger, what are they really showing? They're demonstrating how weak they are. They are taking their fear out on everyone around them, because they're afraid to be real. They get angry, because they don't want to get real. They don't want to get close, so they push people away.

When I am counseling couples, I often see that it's easy for them to argue, disagree, and put up a tough front with each other. There is a lot of complaining, and their defense mechanisms are going strong. It's much more difficult, however, to be intimate and open. Every once in a while, there will be a real tender moment when one of them can finally say to the other that they're scared of losing their partner. For a few moments, there is this window of intimacy. But it's amazing to me how quickly one or both people in the relationship will immediately return to that defensive place.

The purpose behind being willing to be vulnerable is to share for the greater good. If serving our higher purpose means having our personality battered for a while, so be it. It's a very deep issue that most people never even get to, because they're so worried about saving face on the outside they aren't willing to feel what's inside.

Yes, it's a huge risk to let someone see who we are, but it's the most liberating experience in the world. Being willing to tolerate discomfort, being willing to have others disapprove, disagree, or not be pleased with everything that we do and say, to me, is integrity. It is about being real. But we don't always know how to be real. We know how to fight; we know how to be defensive; we know how to protect ourselves. We just don't know how to allow ourselves the opportunity to be tender, real, and risk being vulnerable. We associate vulnerability with something dangerous, yet it's the secret to freedom. Liberation is not caring what other people think of us. It's being able to say: "Okay, this is who I really am. This is my core, my essence. Take it or leave. Either way I'm good."

In the bigger picture, it takes much more strength to show our weaknesses and to say we're battling this or that challenge. People usually don't see our weaknesses, because we have become so adept at covering them up. Crushing our ego means exposing our weaknesses. Would you say to the person, who sits next to you at the office: *I'm jealous of you, because I want the job and the salary that you have?* Probably not, but I bet such an admission would lead to quite an interesting and truthful conversation. To have real relationships, to have a successful marriage, and a loving connection with our kids, we need to be strong enough to admit our weakness.

Seeking Approval

Kabbalist Isaac Luria, the Ari, as he was known, was one of the greatest Kabbalists who ever lived. More then 500 years ago, he talked about soul mates, a topic that fascinates people to this day. One interesting thing he said is that there are certain indicators that reveal if people are soul mates. It is not uncommon that when a couple declares that they want to be married, one or both families are strongly opposed to these people coming together. Strange, huh? Surely if two people have finally met their soul mate, and they're in love and want to spend the rest of their lives together, you'd think the families would be thrilled. Yet the Ari stated that the families often will speak out against the match. They'll say that the person is not good enough, doesn't have enough money, is not educated enough, is divorced, or has kids from a previous marriage. What's the Ari trying to teach us?

For many of us, the most important thing when we decide to get married is our family's blessing. Marriage is one of the most important decisions we'll ever make, so when we finally meet "the one," how could our own family be against it? What a test! If the couple's need for family approval undermines the couple's sense of unity and a genuine belief in their relationship, everything can fall apart. On more than one occasion, I've seen couples walk away from each other because their parents aren't happy.

On the other hand, imagine being able to get past the need for approval, the need to look good in the eyes of others, the need to have your mate be the perfect person from your family's point of view. Many times, it's the willingness on the part of the couple to go against the need for approval and to stand up for their higher purpose—to be with their true soul mate—that's liberating. They're freed of the need for others to like and approve their choice. It's a tremendous test, which is what the Ari was referring to.

In many situations we are given the opportunity to go against the grain, to swim upstream. This is one of the qualities we learn about in leadership: the ability to go against the popular approach and be willing to deal with confrontation and opposition, rejection or approval. What part of us seeks approval? Our ego—the part of us that wants everyone to like us and like what we are doing.

When I was dating my wife, Michal, my father didn't approve of us at all until we set the date for the wedding, just fifty days before we actually got married. He was convinced that maybe there was somebody else better for me in the world. Remember, this man is everything to me—he's not only my father, but my teacher and best friend. Everything he says is like gold. If there was one person in the whole world that I wanted to love my wife, it was my father. For the three and a half years we dated, he was always saying that there might be somebody else, somebody better for me. Part of me always wanted his approval, but part of me said, there is Light waiting to be revealed here and something is going to happen.

Part of what makes our marriage special is that we had to go through the experience of not having our relationship approved by one of the most important people in my life. And it wasn't a secret. A lot of people knew that my father had this opinion. It was embarrassing, but it helped cleanse the ego. Now I know it's because of that period we went through that Michal and I have the kind of special relationship and love we share today.

Enabling other people's egos

It's not only our own ego that causes problems. Part of what we do in order to win approval is to enable someone else's ego. We are so easily impressed with successful people, with celebrities, and power brokers. We admire them. We idealize and idolize them. But what we are really doing is buying into the illusion of their ego and, in the process, comparing and seeing ourselves as less. By doing so we don't help them, and we certainly don't help ourselves.

Being part of someone's entourage is an attempt to seek approval, to try to move up, to get people to like us, and to not feel alone. We suppress our own self-worth so we can enable somebody else's ego, in the hopes that we will glean a moment or two of satisfaction. But when you see somebody walking into a club with fifty people, those people are doing nothing but building that person's ego.

Do you think that any one of those fifty people is actually telling the truth to the star of the entourage? If you're one of those fifty people, you better get out of there, because you're not being truthful to them or to yourself. If we can come to a place where we don't feed other people's egos, we end up crushing our own— which is a good thing, remember? Whatever you do for somebody else works for you. If you are building up their ego, you are also feeding your ego.

We like to live vicariously through other people's successes, because this feeds into our own fantasies. We think that the aura of their success will extend to us somehow. The reality, as we know, is that the celebrities we clamor to see or read about also have insecurities, parenting issues, difficulty setting limits, and trouble dealing with all sorts of judgment from the outside world. What part of us buys into the illusion? Our ego. The ego implants the idea that living through a celebrity or living through our successful friends is an effective way to avoid our own chaos. We put on a false front; we conceal the secret of emptiness; we create a shell around how needy we feel.

Real loyalty, real friendship, is being able to feel the pain of others and to go to hell for them in order to help them go to heaven. We go down, so that they can come up. And they'll do the same for us. Fake loyalty, as in the star in relation to his entourage or vice versa, provides nothing of value to anyone. One-way relationships are pure ego. When there is only one person giving and only one receiving, that's ego at work. In a real friendship, both parties give and take. If it's one way, it's never going to work.

How often do we sell out our friends? How many of your friends have sold you out? How many times did they tell you what you wanted to hear? "You're great. You're honest. You're perfect!" But a real friend is willing to say: "I love you. I care about you. I'm here for you, but you're selfish, you rarely listen, and you really need to deal with your anger. You need to look at your self-absorbed nature to get past it." That is how you truly serve someone. Instead, we feed their egos by saying: "I think you're just fine. Don't change a thing."

The tool of confrontation

When we talk about life without ego, we're talking about being liberated; we're talking about freedom. If we allow people to be who they are, and allow ourselves to be who we are, we have the freedom to relax. We don't have to worry any longer about others' approval. We don't have to like everybody in return, but we do need to have respect for all people, allow others their dignity, and have the patience to allow others to be who they are.

People tell me that I am a very different man now than what I was six or seven years ago. I used to be very, very shy and would rarely reveal myself in public. People who didn't know me well couldn't figure me out. I'm a Gemini with attention deficit challenges and can be all over the place—so they had a lot of judgment. This created distance between me and others. One new student, after about six months at the Kabbalah Centre, was dealing with some issues, including his perception of me, and became so angered and frustrated that he left the Centre for a while. He'd been listening to rumors and gossip. Like attracts like. When your head is filled with garbage, all you do is create an opening for more garbage.

During his months away from the Centre, he was able to appreciate some insights about himself and realize that many of his problems stemmed from getting what he needed instead of what he wanted. He thought he wasn't getting approval from me, when in fact he had judged me before we had a chance to establish a connection. When he finally came back, he started to be more serious about his personal work, changing and taking responsibility for who he was. He started to fall in love with the Centre, and we started to have some interactions.

One day we were at an event together, and he simply came up to me and hugged me. Something had changed. He had become more real and had started to get to know people for who they really are. When we get to know someone we see beneath the façade that people may or may not intentionally show to the world. He managed to see beneath my Attention Deficit Disorder and my apparent craziness. Of course, this allowed me to get to know him, as well. As a result, we formed a strong relationship and now teach workshops together. His ego is no longer in the way.

One of the things the ego relies upon is our tendency to take the easy way out. The ego doesn't want us to confront other people or difficult situations unless it is leading the way. If someone owes you money, you don't want to make the phone call to ask for it back, because you fear that you'll lose that person as a friend. If someone acts inappropriately to you, you have to call them on it. You can't listen to the ego, which is saying: "Oh, don't bother. It's okay." What about the hurt that's inside? If we don't remove the hurt, the relationship can't move forward. Confrontation is a tool given to us by the Universe in order to remove ego, in order to remove the space between people.

We often have a false notion of what personal loyalty to another person means. Our loyalty should be to transform our nature. That is our purpose. It is not about misguided loyalty: being so dependent in your relationship, that you won't tell the truth or call your partner on inappropriate behavior. True loyalty means not allowing someone to get away without paying you back the money he owes you. True loyalty means you will hold the people in your life accountable and not be afraid of a confrontation. Confrontation, by the way, doesn't mean we have to become enraged, intimidating, and bullying. Confrontation simply means being direct. Sometimes, you have to tell someone in a direct way what you're really feeling, what is really going on. That is true accountability.

When we remove the ego, we remove the space between us. Then you and I are one. In the presence of ego, you and I can't be one. We could never be one. So one of the ways to remove space in a relationship is by confronting others over the small things, as well as the big things. Whether the person owes you a million dollars or didn't pick up your shirts from the dry cleaners as promised, it's time to speak up. That's the only way we guarantee that the ego will be removed from the relationship. It doesn't mean it's all right to be nasty; it's not. Do it as nicely as possible. Do it in a loving and caring way, but make sure your point comes across. *You cannot treat me without human dignity. You must treat me with respect.* If we don't call others out on whatever they've done, the Universe ultimately will. And, when the Universe does it, it hurts a lot more.

[Light-Work]

We understand more about ego now, but how do we get rid of it? How do we free ourselves from it? There is no simple, comfortable way to crush the ego, so the Light-Work is not going to be easy. It is exactly what you would expect—to be willing to face the most uncomfortable and embarrassing situations we could possibly encounter. In order to get a taste of what it means to break through the hard shell of the ego, think about a way or two that you could embarrass yourself. If our goal is to be free, we have to be willing to be embarrassed, even to seek embarrassment. I know it sounds crazy, but imagine choosing to become embarrassed. It's such a paradox, but that's what we learn in our spiritual work: to turn into the face of discomfort instead of running away from it.

The Light-Work now is to do something outrageous outside your comfort zone. What can you do to break your sense of being proper and correct? Think outside the box. Do something crazy, *not* dangerous, *not* thrill seeking. That's ego, as well. Be willing to look like a regular schmo. That doesn't mean acting like a jerk. It doesn't mean we have an excuse to be selfish because now we're doing our spiritual work, and it certainly doesn't mean we can humiliate others because it is good for their ego. No, it is not good for their ego. We take care of our ego; they'll take care of theirs.

Put yourself out there and challenge your ego in any way that you know is uncomfortable for you. What can you do to get outside your normal, comfortable life? Be willing to do something that you normally wouldn't do. In order to change, to transform our nature, everything has to be done in reverse. Instead of looking for comfort, we seek discomfort. Instead of looking good, we must be willing to look bad, to look vulnerable, weak, not accomplished, even like a failure.

Come up with something outrageous, the biggest challenge you've faced so far. For example, if you are very quiet and shy and you'd never in a zillion years speak up in a public forum or committee meeting, that is exactly what you need to do. Speak up and risk opening yourself to other people's scrutiny. If you never put your hand up in class, do so. If you've never, ever gotten up there to sing karaoke, this is karaoke week for you. Sing your heart out. If you are uncomfortable dancing, then dance in public. Wear one of those flowery Hawaiian shirts to work, or something that is going to draw attention to you. Someone is bound to ask: "What's the matter with you?" That's exactly the kind of reaction you want to get.

Be willing to be embarrassed. When you confront the greatest amount of fear and ego, you reveal the most Light. You free yourself. I can't think of anything more powerful.

Go back to your journal and see what you've written about experiences in which your ego was crushed. What's it like to immerse yourself in the experience of crushing your ego and embarrassing yourself? How did you feel? What was the experience like for you? Don't go numb. Don't detach. Don't go through the motions. Allow yourself to feel it. It's crucial to feel what it's like to confront those kinds of feelings. That's what this Light-Work is about.

[Additional Light-Work]

Do you want some extra credit? We talked about closeness, about intimacy, and vulnerability—all the proactive experiences on the other side of the ego. When I was in college, it was said that in order to stay happy and healthy, we need to hug twelve people a day. It's one thing to do that in California, but can you imagine doing that in London or Manhattan? The people there barely even look at you. It would be inappropriate and improper there. But imagine if your goal was to hug twelve people today. Imagine the rejection. People will look at you like you're a lunatic.

What if you were to find a way to give a hug to two or three people you don't know, with the emphasis on *giving*? Find a way to open yourself. You have to be friendly, warm. Loosen up. See if you can approach someone, a stranger or someone you don't know very well, and hug them. Make sure this is an appropriate thing to do. I'm not talking about encroaching on people's space and making them uncomfortable. I'm talking about making yourself uncomfortable. Seek out opportunities to give your energy, your kindness, your patience. Maybe you'll let a car in ahead of you during rush hour, if that's something you don't usually do. Take actions that you know will make other people feel good, with no attachment to the results, no expectations. You're not doing it because you need to look good or be validated. You're not going to change someone's life with these actions. Forget about all that. That's ego. Do it because you need to step out of your world of comfort.

It's time to stop making everything about you. Look for opportunities to give to others. Use embarrassment to help you chip away all your blockages and your garbage. Ego is the very debris that you are trying to chip away.

Reactive
& Proactive

Chapter 9
Limitations of Reaction

The last Light-Work you had to do was a bit awkward and uncomfortable—doing something to crush the ego by going out of your comfort zone, doing something that could bring on embarrassment, humiliation, or make you vulnerable and susceptible to other people's judgment or opinions. We need to break the power the ego has to keep us superficial and phony. This is about getting real. If you didn't do the Light-Work, please stop and go back to it. This is one piece of work that you cannot avoid. If you're resisting doing the work, your ego is already controlling you. Break that control.

What Is Reactivity?

When we act without consciousness, in an automatic, knee-jerk fashion, we call that *reactivity*. No thought or effort is involved in our behavior. It's our inflexible response to a situation. If we're hot-tempered, we use angry words. If we're impatient, we act frustrated. If we are feeling insecure, we gossip—even though we know that there are negative consequences to these reactive things we do. Five seconds of reactivity could destroy a relationship with a friend of ten or twenty years.

We feel that our reactive nature is our real nature. We block ourselves from being open or sharing with others because of fear or jealousy. When we feel good about ourselves, we feel *that* is us. But it's simply our reactive behavior, our natural reaction to external stimuli; it's not us at the core. Our reactive behavior is our ego, the Opponent within us, that part of us that tries to keep us receiving for the self alone—which we know now is not the real us. In Kabbalah, reactivity is a code word to describe the nature of the vessel. It's not good or bad; it's simply a direction.

The problem arises when we fail to recognize the connection between the cause and effect of our reactive behavior. How many times have we gotten upset because we're in some kind of a situation, like an accident, and we feel that life is not fair. How often do we find ourselves complaining about injustice in the world? Why? Because our five senses, including our ego, don't recognize the cause behind all the effects. To say something is unfair, "the suddenly syndrome" we talked about previously, means we are not recognizing the cause that produced the effect that has struck us "suddenly." But we can learn to combat the "suddenly syndrome" by recognizing the role that cause and effect play in our actions.

Think about it: How much of our day is taken up by habitual behavior? How much of our life is scripted? We wake up in the morning and go through the motions; we bolt down to breakfast; we race to work, to our errands, to the gym, to the supermarket. How often during the day do we stop and think about what we're doing? Our habits are ingrained in us, which is one of the main reasons we're resistant to spirituality or to Kabbalah. Our habitual behavior would have to change if we recognized and accepted the way universal principles like cause and effect operate. Our robotic consciousness would have to change. We would have to start thinking of what we're doing. It's so much simpler to let our ego control our life. Living a life of reactivity means that we don't have to make any choices; all we have to do is react. But automatic behavior leads to chaos. We become depressed, feel victimized, and are never fulfilled.

Free will

Free will is grossly misunderstood by most people. If you ask someone what they think free will is, they'll tell you it means having the opportunity to make a decision. And nothing could be further from the truth. Free will is not simply: "I'm going to choose one comfortable thing over another." Free will only happens when we go against our reactivity.

One of the ways to recognize when we're being reactive is how easy it is: reactivity requires no effort, discipline, or stretching to get out of our comfort zone. For instance, when we stand in line at a bank, instead of mustering the energy of patience, we complain to the person in front of us about how slow the line is; we fidget or talk on our cell phones. Our reactions are unconscious, and they benefit no one.

Typically, reactive kinds of behaviors or reactions include: resentment, jealousy, pride, insecurity, vindictiveness, vengeance, hatred, wanting to get even, wanting to put someone down. By the way, these are Scorpio-like qualities, and we've all got Scorpio tendencies. We all can be vindictive when we're hurt. We all can be controlling or possessive. We all can be mistrustful or suspicious. But what's interesting about Scorpios is that they're the most loyal, most committed sign of the Zodiac . . . until you cross them. Then, like a scorpion, they'll seek vengeance. That's reactivity. *When I don't understand why you no longer choose to be close to me, I will cut you off because I can't deal with the pain.* Our reactive tendencies are intense, extreme, comfort-seeking, and blaming.

Expectations & Fulfillment

When we look for others to give us fulfillment on any level, we're bound to react, even though no fulfillment will ever come from reactivity. If the seed I'm planting has the DNA of an apple, how could I possibly expect the tree that grows from it to produce an orange? It's impossible. If I plant seeds of doubt, fear, and insecurity, how can I become positive, excited, optimistic, and close? On the other hand, when we look inside for our fulfillment, we are not caught in reactivity, because our internal source of Light will never disappoint us.

One of my favorite stories concerns a kabbalist named Zusha. He didn't give talks or classes and didn't have a community around him; he simply led by example; he taught others indirectly through who he was and how he lived his life. One day, the other spiritual leader in his town knocked on his door at three A.M. This man always felt like Zusha was taking away his students and that people were listening more to Zusha than to him. Zusha was shocked to see him at his home in the middle of the night. The man said, "I have to talk to you. Why don't you care how many students you have? Why don't you care if anyone listens to you? You couldn't care less, and yet you have all these people begging to hear what you have to say. I want to have students, but no one cares what I have to say. I'm more intelligent than you. I dress nicer and look better. Everything about me is better than you. What do you have that I don't?"

Zusha replied, "Remember that wedding three weeks ago?"

The man nodded yes. "Do you remember what happened?"

"Vaguely."

"Let me tell you what happened. The messenger came to invite you. You looked at the list and saw that you were the seventh person invited. You were angry. How dare they invite you seventh? As the most powerful person in town, you needed to be the first on the list. So you decided to show them. You figured they probably wanted you to marry them, so you decided to arrive two hours late. Well, when you arrived, somebody else had already done the ceremony. Okay, you let that go; at least you'd be sitting on the dais with the bride and groom. But someone was already sitting there and you couldn't find another place to sit. You went to the kitchen, asked for some food, and were given a half-eaten piece of chicken, which you ate, and went home—furious, not before cursing out the bride and groom. You cursed out everyone. You couldn't believe that this horror happened to you.

"On the other hand, when the messenger arrived with my invitation, I was so happy to be invited. They're not family; they didn't have to invite me. I went two hours early to see what I could do to help. They even invited me to do the ceremony. They invited me to sit at the dais. I went home and had love in my heart for the whole world. I expected nothing and I got everything. You expect everything and, therefore, get nothing. When you remove your expectations and your sense of entitlement, the Universe offers itself to you."

This direct response was just what that person needed to hear to start him on a spiritual path. Zusha's words prompted him to look at the blockages keeping him from achieving fulfillment, and he later became quite successful as a teacher. Like the man in this story, we can become so involved with what we expect from others, so involved with how others will grant us fulfillment, that we miss the point of life.

What is expectation? It's the idea that something will go a certain way, based on our own terms and our limited understanding and beliefs. If circumstances don't unfold as we imagined, we get upset. "That's not what was supposed to happen," we say. Expectations are a part of the 1 Percent, and they don't require much from us. They stand in stark contrast to a willingness to create what we want to happen, instead of just waiting for results. Expectations are rigid. They contribute to reactivity.

When we're reactive, we often behave insensitively. We're not thinking about the consequences of our hurtful words or the pain we may cause others. We're not thinking about how we may damage the trust in our relationship. We're just taking advantage of what's right in front of our line of sight. We're not sharing our Light; we are only taking energy from others. We victimize others with our reactivity.

Now you are beginning to see the harm in your actions, and when we recognize the destruction we are leaving in our wake, we naturally want to make a change. Later on in this book, we'll talk about the actions we can take to stop our reactive behavior. Right now, we only need to be concerned with noticing the many times each day when we're reactive.

How often do we wake up in the morning and think: "Today is going to be the best day of my life? Today is going to be something special." That's not how we usually think. If we are a Taurus, for example, we might wake up with the same habitual thoughts every morning and wind up having the exact same day every single day. A Taurus might wear the same kind of clothes, go to the same restaurant, and order the same meal. Many of us are stuck in the same kind of pattern. We do the same things every day.

Take a few moments to think about what you could do differently today—and, more importantly, *do it*. Move the couch from one side of the room to the other side. Watch your TV from a different chair. It's okay to start small. Once we dare to begin to do things differently, our life starts to resonate on a new frequency, one that brings Light into our lives. But, when we live on the same old frequency and do the same old things every day, we're not really living. We're dead. And a dead person will never find fulfillment. The ego and its reactive nature want things to remain the same. Why? If we change, we could let the Light in, and that's the last thing that the ego wants!

When you wake up tomorrow morning, say: "Today is going to be different than any other day." Sign up for a yoga class. Speak to someone on the street. Take a different route to work. Ask the new employee in your office to lunch. There is no end to the new things you can try today.

[Light-Work]

What would make today a great day, even if nothing exciting actually happened? We're not getting married today, or throwing our best friend a birthday party. We're not going out to the bar or a movie; we have nothing planned to look forward to. But we can still have a great day by breaking free from our habitual bubble. We may be waking up to the same partner, with the same kids, but we're choosing to make today different by not being reactive. In other words, whatever it is you do today, do it consciously, with awareness. Inject energy, a sense of meaning and purpose, into whatever it is you choose to do.

Think about your typical drive to work, one that is usually made unconsciously, reactively. We drive through our neighborhood, get on the freeway, and head to our office. Have we paid any attention to all the turns we've had to make? All the stop signs at which we stopped? Rarely. We're usually doing multiple things at once: listening to the radio, on the phone, driving. We're usually on autopilot and completely oblivious. The problem, however, with multitasking is that we miss being connected to our present experience.

Most of us have to drive to work if we want to pay the rent. But we have a choice in how we do it, how much energy we put into it. Yes, there will always be parts of our life that are stuck in habit, but even our habitual world can be different if we choose to inject energy into it. Every action, even if it's the same one every day, can contain some special quality. If we focus on that, then our life is alive and not dead.

Brainstorm all the situations in which you're moving through your day on autopilot. Maybe it's in the way you get up and out of bed, the way you dress, the way you have your breakfast, when you leave to go to work, or the route you take. When you get to work, who do you speak to? What kind of energy do you put into your work? Do you do just the bare minimum? How many times does someone say: "Hi, how are you?" And you always answer: "Fine, how are you?" Is your response a thoughtful one? Do you care about the answer you will receive?

Driving is a great way to learn about reactivity. Watch how angry or agitated we become while behind the wheel. Watch how our selfish nature rears its head. Notice how often we don't want to let anyone in front of us. Would the drive go more smoothly for us and the other driver if we let the person into our lane? Think about these questions and write down your answers. When you begin to see the limitations of your reactive nature, you will see the need for an overhaul.

Chapter 10

Power of Discomfort

Did you have a great day, or at least decide how you will make your next day special and different? That was your Light-Work. It was designed to help you see outside the scope of your reactive, habitual nature. Don't worry—we all have this side to our nature. And it has the potential to lead to chaos.

In order to master chaos, we have to truly grasp what it means to be in it. The first step of Kabbalah is to admit and identify our chaos, ego, and reactivity. Stay open and focused now, as we delve more into the notion of reactivity.

Reactivity

Everyone is challenged by anxiety, fears, depression, phobias, addictions—you name it! What you may not realize is that all forms of anxiety, fear, and depression are purely reactive states. There is nothing proactive about them. Let's consider the fight-or-flight response for a moment. We're all governed by this mechanism of the autonomic nervous system. If you are shocked, traumatized, or in some kind of danger, your system produces a burst of adrenaline. Blood rushes to the limbs; hormones are secreted. You get an extra power boost to fight off the bear or the burglar and get the hell away. You don't even have to make this difficult decision consciously; it's done for you.

The problem arises when that reactive fight-or-flight response is triggered in inappropriate settings. If you're dealing with a natural disaster, a little adrenaline boost can go along way. Having this extra strength can save lives. But when you get a phone call from the IRS or your bills are overdue, and your body is responding as if you were in the middle of an earthquake, then it's time to pause for a moment. Your physiology is controlling you; this is pure reactivity. Some forms of anxiety and fear can certainly serve a purpose. But we have lost our ability to decide how we will respond to the fear.

Think of a smoke alarm. Would you say a smoke alarm is good or bad? It depends if it's working, right? If it's working effectively, a smoke alarm is a warning detection system that can save your life. Hopefully, you hear the alarm and attend to the problem. But let's say the smoke alarm battery doesn't work, or somebody cut the wires. This disconnect has the potential to lead to some very bad consequences. In the same way, our fight-or-flight mechanism can be incredibly helpful, but if it isn't working properly or is overworked, it loses its effectiveness.

There are two ways to understand reactivity. We can overreact: get too angry, be too judgmental, or too critical of others. But it's also possible that we shut down completely, become disconnected, or depressed. Becoming numb is a way in which we try to protect ourselves from getting hurt. This is often connected to traumatic memories from our past. Wherever the fear is coming from, our numbness is preventing us from being alive and functioning optimally today. In this way, both overreacting and shutting down are forms of reactivity.

This reminds me of a joke about two guys in a mental institute. They have a plan of escape, and they're going to meet at nine o'clock to make a break for it. One guy is in charge of supplies; the other is in charge of figuring out how to get over the wall. They decide together that if the wall is six feet or over, they're going to build a tunnel. If it's six feet or less, they're going to find a way to jump over.

Nine o'clock comes and they meet up. "So, did you get the supplies?" The one man asks.

The other responds, "Yes, but I have some bad news. We're in here for life."

"Why do you say that?"

"Well we can't dig a tunnel or jump over the wall because there is no wall. We're stuck."

We behave just like these two men when we think we can't move on and shut ourselves down. The result is a self-imposed prison.

Fear and Anxiety

A number of years ago, an amazing research study at Pennsylvania University showed that close to 78 percent of the U.S. population spends up to eight hours a day dealing with fear and worry. And around 40 percent of the stuff that we worry about will never happen.

Thirty percent is taken up with thoughts and distortions of situations from our past—events that we can't change. Twelve percent of what we worry about is other people's business. For example, your parents might obsess over what's happening with you in school or worry about your lifestyle. Ten percent of what we worry about is what's considered to be imagined illness: Our flu is turning into pneumonia, and our pneumonia into cancer; we read about a new type of virus and find ourselves worrying that we have contracted it.

Do the math—92 percent of our worries are reactive. Ninety-two percent! That leaves 8 percent of fear or worry that's justifiable.

Here's a simple example. If you are about to run across a busy street, you'll want to look both ways. It's a wise, healthy thing to do, because you could get hit by a car if you don't. The risk is real. You wouldn't choose to stick your finger in a light socket because you know the chance that you'll get shocked is very high. So to say that all fear is reactive is not true. Reactive fears are those that control us, those that cause us to panic and handle our situations inappropriately.

By the way, if you're someone who has panic attacks, chances are you've ended up in the emergency room thinking you were having a heart attack. It's terrifying. Why did your body and mind respond in such an extreme way? Because you didn't attend to the smoke alarm that was going off a few weeks ago, which said: *Attend to your financial situation. Deal with your relationship conflict. Deal with your health. Listen to what the doctor is telling you about your diet.* We can choose to handle these minor inconveniences of life proactively. Or we can wait for chaos to unfold before we do anything, which leads to quite a rollercoaster ride—including possible trips to the Emergency Room. Life becomes a constant up and down. You wake up fearful and wondering: *What is life going to bring me today?* It is a scary, over-stimulating, and potentially Soul-destroying way of living. It's pure reactivity.

Depression

We can allow our fears to close us off from the world. We can become paralyzed as we fall deeper and deeper into blame and depression. We feel isolated and alone, and nobody would choose to feel this way—not consciously anyway. Nobody would choose to feel insecure. Who wants to look in the mirror and beat themselves up because of the wrinkles they see or the weight they've gained? Nobody in their right mind would choose that! So how do we end up in such pain? Because we have allowed reactive seeds in our unconscious mind to grow.

An anxiety or panic attack is the result of a reactive seed that we have planted in the past. It can grow into a specific fear or a fear that is vague, but just as undermining to our well-being. This is called "generalized anxiety," and it means we don't have a clue as to why we're anxious. I used to call it the "Woody Allen Syndrome"—walking around neurotic, worrying about everything. It's part of that 92 percent of unfounded fears. Needless to say, a person walking around like this is not in control of his or her life.

Depression is just as painful as anxiety, and it is often greatly misunderstood. Depression does not always manifest as sadness; it is often a state of feeling nothing. It's numbness, no desire at all. In order for Light to be revealed in our life, there has to be a vessel to contain it. We have to have a desire. We have to want something before we can bring it into our life. The problem with depression is that we have no desire. We can barely get out of bed. We might be alive and breathing, but we feel nothing. This state seems like it would be the furthest from reactivity since we are taking no action at all, but actually it is a form of reactive living.

Once I had to speak at a funeral. I asked my father, "Dad, what can I do to bring some Light into this darkness?" He said, "The truth is that life and death have nothing to do with the person living or dying. Most of us have people alive next to us, but for us they're dead, either because we've shut down or they've shut down. If we've had a great relationship with someone, even when they pass on, they're still alive for us. So, it's really up to us to determine whether someone who leaves this world will be dead or alive for us. Just as it is our choice whether we want to be alive or dead."

Talk about an answer that gave me some perspective! I started seeing the people in my life quite differently. We have to choose to be alive, to be part of this game of life. You can either play the game or not. You always have a choice.

Coming out of the darkness

We've learned to recognize the darkness and diagnose it. We can see it, feel it, taste it, and are beginning to understand it. So how do we come out of the shadows? First, it is helpful to take a few moments and figure out what parts of our life are alive and which parts are dead. Who have we shut out? How have we shut down? We've talked about numbness, depression, anxiety, fear—all of our reactive qualities. Now, it's time to shed some real Light on these subjects.

What happens when you turn on the light in a dark room? The darkness disappears. There are parts of our life that are exactly like this dark room, and one of the ways we can add brightness is by using the tool of restriction. We talked earlier about being able to pause, to stop and identify when we're starting to become reactive. Now we have to move into the next phase: how can we move out of our natural reactive tendency into a more proactive effort?

If you try to pour five pints of beer into a one-pint glass, it simply won't be able to contain all that beer. It's going to spill over—just like the tea that the Zen Master poured into the student's cup. Like the cup, we, too, can become flooded. We become overwhelmed, saturated, and reactive. Restriction is the point at which we start to take control over our reactive nature. It's holding ourselves accountable for the amount of energy that pours into our vessel.

Restriction is a bit like a thermostat. A thermostat keeps the temperature of the room accountable to a specific temperature. There is nothing more frustrating than being in a room where the thermostat doesn't work. You're constantly getting up to adjust the temperature. Our free will, like the thermostat, is a valve that regulates our spiritual temperature. It is designed to regulate how much energy we're drawing in and how much energy we're sharing; how much attention we're giving to our partners and how much attention we're demanding from them. How much love, care, and tolerance we're giving others and how much tolerance we are requiring from them. Restriction allows us to become a reasonable person, one who consciously chooses the thoughts we allow to linger in our minds and the words that flow from our mouths.

It's important that we tell our friends the truth, even if it means that they won't like what we have to say. But, according to Kabbalah, there are a couple of criteria that must exist before we begin. First of all, they must have a genuine desire to hear our opinions. There needs to be a vessel. If you tell someone what you think of them but they're closed and unreceptive, our sagely advice does them no good. If this is the case your need to get your thoughts off your chest is nothing more than a selfish, reactive desire. Your wanting to share your opinions is a form of venting or an attempt to alleviate your own guilt. The desire on their part to hear what we have to say must exist first and foremost.

Secondly, there has to be real care and trust between these two people. Part of becoming accountable, of restricting our reactive nature, is to consider the other person's ability to receive our words. I can tell you, I've made some mistakes. I confronted people before they were ready. I have unintentionally insulted others, because they were not quite ready to trust my intentions. As a result, I learned that I couldn't talk to everyone the same way. Some people need to hear things in a very gentle, elliptical way, while other people require directness and straight talk.

I'll give you an example. Someone born under the sign of Cancer is very sensitive. It would be a mistake to criticize a Cancer directly; they will become very uncomfortable and shut down. They can't take it. You have to be gentle and build trust with them. You have to tell them your concerns in a roundabout way. But, a Sagittarius or Scorpio has no patience for sugar-coating. They want you to tell it like it is. The lesson here is that we can't have a cookie-cutter approach; we need to adapt ourselves to other people. Sensitivity to others is a proactive quality that requires effort, thought, and awareness.

This reminds me of the story of the kabbalist who had a meeting with someone who sought his advice. When the meeting was finished, his assistant came in and found the kabbalist was soaking wet, as if he had just run a marathon or worked out hard for an hour and a half. The assistant asked, "What happened? Why are you soaking wet?"

The kabbalist said, "You don't understand. From where I sit, the questions of the people I meet with are pointless. The questions they ask would not even be questions for me. In order to overcome this and in order to provide meaningful answers, what I have to do is 'wear their clothing.' I imagine myself in their situations and answer from where they are, not from where I am. And it's hard work!"

Unfortunately, we rarely do this. We speak to people from where we're at—either speaking down to them or over their heads. Or we don't even address them at all. We're really speaking to ourselves with somebody else in the room. If we care about someone and want to give something of value to them, we have to put ourselves wholly into their shoes; we have to wear their clothing.

The thermostat reminds me of a lesson I learned from my father when we were in New York right after 9/11. He said, "Unfortunately, people now are very reactive in their spirituality." Everyone was hugging each other. Everyone was nice to each other. New Yorkers typically don't stop on the street to say hello but after 9/11, the city was different. However without special effort, this reactivity never grows into consistent proactivity. Today it's as if 9/11 never happened, and we have largely gone back to our old ways.

Unfortunately, spirituality is often reactive. It's like a thermostat that is on 71 or 72 degrees. When it gets warmer, the air-conditioning clicks on in response. Likewise, we run to spirituality for a solution when the pain gets a little too tough to bear. Finding a solution can be very proactive, but if we are only seeking it because the pain has become too much, then we are approaching it from a reactive consciousness. We can learn to proactively lower our own thermostat, without having to sweat it.

Some people come to the Kabbalah Centre out of pain. Eventually, the ones who just want to remove their pain stop their study. What we hope is that everyone will continue to study, even if there is no active pain, in order to achieve the final destination of total true fulfillment.

Justification

Greatness is not how much we achieve, but how much we overcome. We justify feeling insecure, inadequate, and why we think we'll never amount to anything. We justify our fear of abandonment and our belief that no good will come into our life. We look for validation for our anger, reasons for why we deserve to feel outraged. Where is the justification coming from, anyway? It's coming purely from the ego. The ego allows us to fulfill our negative prophesies again and again, because that's the seed that we have planted—a seed of doubt, fear, and negativity. So, of course that's what we're going to grow as our tree. We're growing a tree of chaos and fear and digging a huge hole at the same time. Is there any other response but to be outraged? Is this really the only way to handle a situation, by causing more chaos?

Of course not. Chaos is NOT the only way. This is good and bad news. The bad news is that in order to avoid chaos, we have to be on our guard—aware and conscious every moment that we're living. We have to choose life every second. We have to insure that our free will is active in every moment. We have to be sure not to slip into automatic behavior, not to be reactive: not just be the effect. Every moment, we have to be the cause for what happens in our life. That's also the good news. Being proactive, taking control over our reactivity, controlling our ego, taking control over our fears, insecurities, doubts and phobias means we can start to experience happiness.

Can we cut darkness out? No. What we can do is transform it. We can illuminate the room with light and the darkness disappears.

[Light-Work]

Let's do some Light-Work to pull all of these ideas together. Think of an example of when you went against your reactive nature today. Or did you remain in reactive mode for most of the day? Did you find yourself being sarcastic or snapping at someone? Did you listen to the tone of your voice and hear ego creeping in? Maybe you were able to turn reactive behavior into proactive behavior while you were stuck in traffic. Were you able to say to yourself: "Yes, I'm late and the traffic is bad, but instead of sitting here with my blood pressure rising, I am going to use this time to listen to some relaxing music and plan my day." Write down in your journal the ways in which you have been able to go against your reactive nature. Write down the ways in which you revealed Light today with your proactive responses.

If you really want to explore on a deeper level some of the personal issues you are experiencing, you can call our toll free number and talk to one of our Kabbalah instructors at 1-800-KABBALAH. Let them know that you're reading *Living Kabbalah*. They'll be excited about helping you. They'll know what kind of journey you're on and how committed and dedicated you must be to get through even the first ten chapters of this book.

Now, remember, when you ask for help you are bringing a great deal of Light into a dark room. Imagine sunlight shining through the windows; when the sun comes in, the sunbeams illuminate the motes of dust in the air. It's an appropriate metaphor for what happens when you begin to bring Light into your life. Immediately, we start to see the garbage. We start to see our negativity. But only when we can see the debris, can we remove it.

Think of it like housekeeping. When we vacuum the carpet, we're looking for dirt to suck up. We don't usually look at dirt on a carpet and go into hysterics about how it got there. There is no need to judge, no need to feel discouraged. There is every reason to keep looking for ways to clean up our negativity and come out of darkness. Keep moving forward.

Chapter 11
Finding the Meaning

How did you do? Did you identify some ways in which you practiced restriction? Was there a time when you wanted to shout but chose to listen instead? Or, maybe there was a moment when you decided to choose a piece of gum instead of smoking a cigarette. Did you feel your Soul lighten when you chose the proactive route? As always, if you didn't do your Light-Work, please stop and go back. This is when tremendous shifts in perspective begin to happen.

Looking for Deeper Meaning

What is the deeper meaning behind the opportunities we have to transform? Let's start connecting some dots.

So many times in our lives, we start on a path and we have absolutely no idea if we're on the right one. It may not even look like we're on any path at all, but eventually we find the meaning.

The dots become connected. Kabbalah not only helps us to figure out the meaning of events in our past, but it helps us understand the deeper meaning of events as they unfold in our present. We know there are no accidents. The movie we are in is not the wrong movie. This is not a mistake. So, if the Creator has brought us this situation as an opportunity, what are we going to do about it?

In Kabbalah, and many places in the *Zohar*, the word Creator is used instead of God because that's our purpose: we came to this world to be a creator. When we're in a reactive state, we're not creating anything. We're not any more creative than a cockroach. But when we upgrade and become a proactive being, restricting our reactive nature, we become creators.

There's a classic story we use in Kabbalah to illustrate the need to rise to our full potential as creators. A popular kabbalist who wrote many books gave a party after finishing one of his books. At the party, he told a story. When he was fourteen years old, he was in bed at night when he overheard a conversation between his parents. "What are we going to do with our boy? He's not successful at school. He's not successful in his studies. Maybe we should put him into a school where he could learn to be a carpenter, something that's useful." After he heard that conversation, the boy changed his life. He started taking his spiritual work and his studies seriously and became one of the greatest kabbalists in history.

Now, of course there is nothing wrong with being a carpenter, but it was in his DNA to be an extraordinary teacher. If he hadn't heard that conversation, he would have left this world thinking that he had fulfilled his potential by being a carpenter. But the angels would have said: "Where are your books? Where are your students?" He would have said: "What are you talking about? I'm a carpenter. I don't have students. I don't have books." They would have shown him his alternative life, where he had many books and students and was fulfilled.

At his party, he said: "I'm thankful today—not for the books I wrote or my status. I'm thankful for being awake that night when my parents had that conversation."

Many times in life we hear casual conversations. We hear some-body say something to a friend of ours that resonates within us. Imagine if we expanded our radar even further. Instead of just looking at those things that happen to us or near us, we could look all around. Imagine the messages we would hear that were meant for us. When we start becoming more proactive beings, we pick up messages from all around us that resonate in our Soul. And, we start to connect the dots a lot quicker.

We all have to leave this world one day. The veil of the five sens-es will be removed and there will be no more limitations, no edit-ing of what we see and feel, no more veils. We will be able to see all the opportunities we had and never took. Imagine if you could have met your soul mate two or three times, but, because you stayed in a bad relationship, because you were afraid of being alone, you never got to meet him or her. Imagine the opportuni-ties you would have had in business if you had invested instead of pulling out. If you had taken more responsibility, taken the management position, gone with the promotion. But you shied away from it and missed becoming a success in business. Imagine if you could see the hurt that you caused others with your offhand comments. You had no idea that you caused them pain, but now you can see why people stopped trusting you, stopped returning your phone calls. Imagine how painful this would be. The lesson is this: Why wait until we leave this world? What if we could actually look for those opportunities now?

The Creator gives us opportunities to take the initiative to transform situations. Placing blame on other people or external situations gets us nowhere. It's not about being a victim. Every challenge, every obstacle, has a specific purpose for us. Remember, there is Light concealed behind every challenge. Our choice is to either react to the event and miss the possibility of revealing that Light, or to confront the challenge head on, proactively, and reveal the Light that's there for all to see.

Why do our buttons get pushed?

Why do we get upset when someone is late all the time? Why do we become impatient around a certain friend? Why do we constantly feel criticized and blamed by others? We all have buttons that get pushed by one person or another. But as long as we're busy blaming that person, we will never change that reactive pattern into Light.

What if you saw your nemesis as someone who was there to help you grow? What if they knocked on your door and said: "Hey, I've been sent here as a messenger to remind you to deal with your anger. I'm going to do something to push your anger button so that you have an opportunity to choose." Would you get angry, or would this prompt you to find another way to handle the situation?

If we could recognize people as messengers of the Light, would we be so insulted by them? We'd be more likely to say: "Wow, thanks. I had no idea." Do we get upset with the UPS guy if we made a mistake and ordered the wrong thing in the catalog? Do we shoot the messenger? Absolutely. That's what we do. That's what our ego does. We blame the messenger, yet, ultimately, where is the message coming from? The Light—which means that the message is, without a doubt, worth hearing.

One of our Kabbalah students had a major life-changing experience twenty years ago. He had just graduated college and moved to Los Angeles from Spain. It was the first time he had experienced a life of freedom. One day he was driving with a friend up Sunset Boulevard to go see Elton John in concert. They had a lot of time to kill, so they pulled into a restaurant to grab some food. A very striking hostess seated them, and our friend started to flirt with her. Not long after this first encounter did it develop into a relationship before he discovered she actually had a big problem with cocaine.

At the time, he was pretty naïve, and he was not involved in drugs of any kind. When his girlfriend said she'd been in rehab a couple of times for cocaine, it meant nothing to him, because she never did cocaine when he was around. Within weeks, he had moved in with this woman, who was fully into a free-base crack cocaine habit. She would disappear for days at a time. He was embarrassed, ashamed, and confused. When she went back into rehab, he discovered how chaotic his relationship with this woman really was.

It was a painful, scary time, and a major awakening. He started learning about alcohol and drug addiction, thinking that his love would be enough for her to stop using. So he went to UCLA and became a certified alcohol and drug counselor. Why? Because of one stop on Sunset Blvd on the way to an Elton John concert.

He could have seen this experience as justification for becoming a victim, for not trusting women, for judging anyone who ever had any involvement with drugs and alcohol. Instead, this very upsetting and painful relationship became a turning point in his life. Now he sees how the Creator gave him the most amazing gift, an opportunity to learn and to change his life completely.

What's Good for the Goose

You know the Light-Work we did a few chapters ago in which you were asked to have someone tell you what they really think about you? Well, it's not the first time I have given this assignment. Not long ago, I gathered our staff together for a workshop. I requested that each staff member in attendance ask someone in the room what they really thought about them. Make sure you love them. Make sure they love you. Let go of any barriers that exist.

I felt good about that exercise. People were opening up. Afterwards, I was traveling in a car with someone and I told him about the exercise. He looked at me and asked: "Who did you go to?"

I said, "I didn't do it myself. I just asked our staff to do it. I was there to lead the class."

He said, "You can't tell people what to do and not do it yourself."

That was uncomfortable to hear. But that's not where the story ends. That night, I went home, turned on my computer, and received an instant message from someone from the workshop who asked: "Can I talk to you?" And he started telling me something that was hard for him to say but felt he had to tell me. He nailed me. He said, "You can't go hot and cold. People think you're always there, but then you go cold on them."

It blew me away. I'm a Gemini; I like excitement. When things aren't exciting, I shut down. I am very hot and cold with people. I was in a cold phase with this person and he called me on it. Because of what my friend had said in the car, I was open to hear this person's criticism. It was as if the uncomfortable part in the car, admitting that I wasn't open to feedback, got me to the place where I was open enough to hear what this other person said.

We have to be able to listen if we want to learn how we affect others, and if we are going to change. Am I totally different person now? Of course not. But I'm working on myself. Since then, it has been easier for me to open myself up for people to tell me things.

And I feel people are more willing to listen to what I have to say to them.

[Light-Work]

Think about somebody who hurt you recently. Now, imagine that the Opponent has hypnotized this person. The Opponent is right next to that person, who is saying, word by word, what the Opponent is prompting him to say. It's not the person talking; it's really the Opponent. That person is a puppet that's being controlled by the Opponent. Do you get angry at the puppet? No. You know it's the Opponent. You know that person is no longer in control. How do you feel about this person now?

In a moment, I'll ask you to look at a situation in life where someone has done something rotten to you, or something that didn't go exactly as you would have liked it to go. There was a lesson to be learned in this experience. Do you know what it was?

Sometimes we don't know the full story or see the whole picture; we don't always know why people are behaving as they are. We don't know the actual meaning of the events unfolding around us. Things aren't always as they seem. It could look like a duck and smell like a duck, but still be a chicken or a bear.

When something especially unpleasant or uncomfortable happens, we could make excuses for it. We could blame others. We could blame ourselves. Maybe we didn't get a good night's sleep or hadn't prepared enough. We could come up with a thousand reasons why things happened the way they did. Alternatively, we could say: "What am I supposed to learn from this situation?" This slight shift in thinking can unveil some incredible lessons.

Speak with someone who has battled cancer. Some cancer survivors will tell you that having cancer was the best thing to ever happen to them. I know many people who went through the some of the darkest times that a person can experience, yet they look back on the experience positively because of the lessons they learned.

It's up to us. We can spend all day talking about how a certain obstacle in our life keeps us down. Or we can figure out *why* that obstacle is there, find the meaning, learn the lesson, move on, and become a better being. Yes, chaos may happen. Unfortunate events may happen. The key is not to get sidelined by them, but instead to find the meaning in them, so that instead of bringing more chaos, they bring fulfillment. When we do this, we reveal more Light for ourselves; more of our true selves becomes activated. If we don't have challenges we cannot experience our full potential, and all of the Light the Creator has to offer us. Events happen in our lives so that we can get to a deeper, more authentic level of living.

The greater the challenge, the more Light we can reveal. But effort is required; there is no way around it. The greater the obstacle, the greater the effort we have to make in order to overcome the obstacle. So, when something happens to you that you don't like, ask yourself: *What lesson am I learning? What's the benefit of this? Why is this in my movie?* Then find a way to overcome this challenge. I guarantee you won't regret the effort.

Remember, Light is concealed in both day-to-day challenges and tragedies. Someone was riding in a cab in New York when the cab driver stopped abruptly to avoid hitting someone. The passenger hit his head on the glass partition in front and had to go to the Emergency Room for stitches. When he went to the Emergency Room, he sat through hours of waiting to be seen by a doctor. They did a scan and discovered this person had a brain tumor, which they were able to remove successfully, because the doctor had found it early enough. Because of this taxi accident, the person survived brain cancer. The accident, which was certainly a challenge, turned out to be a miracle. That is how the Universe can work for us, if we allow it to do so.

[Light-Work]

For your Light-Work, write in your journal an example of a crisis, challenge, or experience that was uncomfortable, painful, or difficult. And ask yourself the questions: *What was the lesson? What was the deeper meaning?* When you find the deeper meaning, you also find the Light.

IV. Reactive & Proactive

Chapter 12
Tools for Proactivity

Our previous lesson had us looking at the challenges in our life and their hidden meanings. Were you able to uncover meaning in some of the hurdles you are facing? Did you write them down? The act of writing and the Light-Work—when done with the intention to reveal truth—can reveal immense Light. If you haven't done the Light-Work, please stop now and complete the previous exercise.

Proactive Behavior

The opposite of reactive behavior is proactive behavior. Proactivity has to do with action, while reactivity is passive in nature; it is a reflex that requires almost no effort at all, no thought, no consciousness. Proactivity is the opposite. It's a choice we make. It is an exercise of our free will. It's asking: *How am I going to handle this situation? Why is this happening? Is it serving me to act this way?*

I'll give you a very profound example. I've had the opportunity to work with many expectant mothers. These pregnant mothers say to me: "I'm really concerned that I might mess up my kid." They have usually survived some pretty awful childhoods themselves. I say, "Let me ask you a question. Don't you think your parents asked that same question before they brought you into this world? It was first and foremost on their minds, too. They wondered how their actions were going to be to your benefit." Just by asking the question, we open ourselves to the opportunity to be proactive and to choose our actions.

But it will require effort. As the vessel, our inherent nature is to be reactive. Everything that involves proactivity is a transformation, a change in our inherent nature. If we are only five feet tall, can we take a pill and grow ten inches taller? Of course not. If our DNA indicated we would be short in stature, we would have to change that DNA before we were born if we hoped to be tall as an adult. Likewise, in trying to change our nature from reactive to proactive, we have to get to the core of our actions. Only when we plant proactive seeds can we begin to change our nature.

When we come into this world, our spiritual DNA is perfect. We are spiritually outfitted to have the best life possible, the most fulfillment and joy conceivable. So what happens? Because of our reactive behavior, we start undermining our divine DNA. When we choose reactivity, we are choosing a life of physical, spiritual, emotional, and mental chaos. The only way to ensure our fulfillment, happiness, and success is by being proactive.

There is a great proverb about a Cherokee wise man imparting a lesson to his grandchildren. He tells them of a fierce battle raging inside each of them, which he likens to a terrible struggle between two wolves. The black wolf represents all things horrific—anger, hatred, fear, sorrow, regret, greed, self-pity, false pride, lies. The white wolf stands for love, hope, happiness, generosity, peace, humility, compassion, and truth. The children ask, "Which wolf wins?" And the wise man answers: "The one you feed." What a perfect illustration! If we feed the ego, we give energy to all those reactive qualities (sorrow, regret, insecurity, anger, hatred) and, if we feed our proactive nature, we give energy to the compassion, gratitude, love, and sharing that exists in our hearts. That's the choice we face: to feed the white wolf or to feed the black wolf.

And it's not over in a day. Imagine the Tour de France; three grueling weeks of cycling with a combination of mountain stages, sprints, and rest days. Getting through the race requires preparation and strategy. Our path, in this life, is just like the Tour de France or any other contest that requires training, effort, and perseverance. When we go on the spiritual path, on the proactive path, we have to train ourselves. We have to be ready. We have to know the obstacles facing us and formulate a strategy.

You are in the process of receiving the necessary training. Some days will be grueling, and you'll wish you had never heard of spirituality. You'll hear things that you don't want to hear and do things you won't want to do. Training for any game or sport is no cake walk. You have to build new muscles and that requires some discomfort. But some days will be easier than others. You might even get some rest days. You can look forward to those. The best days, though, are the days when we see results from our hard work.

How to Choose Proactivity Over Reactivity

Sometimes it is not easy to recognize the difference between reactive and proactive actions or behavior. But if we were to write a list of all the possible reactive traits and all the possible proactive traits, some interesting things emerge. For example, some reactive qualities might be impatience, anger, judgment, blame, and being a victim. What are some proactive qualities? Exactly the opposite.

If we're reactively impatient, to be proactive we have to become patient. If we're reactively judgmental, to be proactive we have to become tolerant and accepting. If we're selfish on the reactive side, we need to be generous on the proactive side.

What are some typical situations that trigger reactivity, and what might the proactive solutions be? Let's talk about telemarketers—everyone can relate to the topic of telemarketers. Every day someone calls our home trying to sell us the *L.A. Times*. It's amazing how this can trigger complete belligerence in the person who is being called. There is a very simple solution to handling someone who is trying to sell you something when you're busy, and you feel like they're invading your space: try to figure out a way to give them a blessing. Share your time. Give them just one minute, be patient and considerate, gently let them know you are not interested. Make the situation less about you and more about them.

IV. Reactive & Proactive

Remember, they're a messenger. Is their solicitation meant to be taken personally? Are they trying to hound you and make your life hell? Not usually. The person making the call is simply trying to earn a living. This is what they do. And the product they're trying to sell you may even be meaningful to them. Remember, there are no accidents, no coincidences—just opportunities. The phone call is really just the Creator saying: "Hey, remember, you have to deal with your intolerance problem. You have to deal with your judgments. You have to deal with those loose lips and the way that you can be rude to people."

Another example is traffic. You're sitting in a taxi in a new city. You have no control over the slow pace of the rush-hour traffic or the driver's unusual taste in music. Instead of becoming upset and mouthing off at the driver, take a moment to appreciate the scenery. Take out that book you have wanted to start. Tell the driver a funny joke you heard recently. Remember that the reason you feel agitated is because your buttons are being pushed, and this experience is precisely what you need to transform your reactive behavior into Light.

Certainty

One of the things that we discover from Kabbalah is that doubt can be seen as the root of all negativity. If there is one thought that will determine a negative, chaotic outcome, it is doubt. Doubt prevents us from ever making a positive change. You doubt whether you'll ever be able to have a good relationship; you doubt if you can be a success in business. We have to have proof before we take action, right? A large percentage of our thoughts are based upon *what if*. But when we live in the world of *what if*, we only ensure chaos.

What is the opposite of doubt? *Certainty*. Certainty is not about faith, wishful thinking, or good intentions. Certainty, according to Kabbalah, is the ultimate proactive tool, because it is about action. Anything to do with proactivity is active. When certainty is present, we allow ourselves to risk, to break out of what we believe is our comfort zone, in spite of the doubt we might feel.

The Creator doesn't always give us everything that we ask for because we don't always know what's best for us. When we pray, "Please, God, make this person my soul mate," the Creator might respond by saying: "What, are you kidding? Don't you see what's coming six months from now? You don't see the deception in this person? Of course not, you're too taken by his good looks and charm. But, a few months from now, when you learn more about his character, you'll see this is not someone you should be so enamored of." Certainty means believing that the Creator has our best interests at heart. It means that we might have to let go of our own expectations about how things should be.

Certainty requires filtering out the negative thoughts that foster fear and doubt. Remember that we are bombarded with thoughts from two sources, two radio stations: that of the Light and that of the Opponent. Our job is to be sure which radio station we're tuning into. If you are picking up on a signal that is prompting doubt in your heart, you are not tuning in to the right station.

Some people call this attitude of doubt "healthy skepticism." That's like having a healthy anger problem or a healthy addiction. There is nothing healthy about skepticism, because the root of skepticism is doubt. Is it helpful to be open to seeing the big picture? Sure. But that's not skepticism. It's okay to have questions; Kabbalah encourages them. But there is a difference between asking questions and being willing to dig deeper to find honest answers before we draw any conclusions: that's certainty.

This concept of certainty is an important quality of proactivity. Certainty is what we activate when we decide to face a challenge and confront our ego. Someone who has complete certainty in an outcome allows no room for their reactive nature. Certainty erases anything that could make this person fail. Certainty gives doubt no room to breathe. But the second there is even the smallest puncture in that certainty, the floodgates open. You can't have eighty percent certainty. It's still doubt. Ninety-nine percent certainty still makes room for doubt. Only by having complete certainty can we shut down our reactive, doubting system.

We all know people who are convinced of doom and gloom. You know the kind of person I'm talking about. They walk around with a dark cloud hovering over them, saying: "Woe is me. You're going to leave me. Everything is going to go wrong." This person lives in complete doubt. But, you know what's amazing about it? You know what system they're really using? You know what they're proving? The power of Certainty. By being certain that doom and gloom will come, this person is ensuring that they will. Imagine if they could transform that negative consciousness into positive consciousness and use the same power of certainty to create goodness in their life!

It All Depends on You

There is a story about a kabbalist who lived during a time of war. A student came to him and said: "I have to cross the border. I must see my father; he's dying, and we have unfinished business. Please help me."

The kabbalist went inside his office and came back out an hour later and said: "Here, I've done it." He handed the student a piece of paper and said: "Fold this up, give it to the crossing guard. Everything will be okay."

The student left, opened the note, and saw a blank piece of paper. He said, "There is no way that I'm going to give a blank piece of paper to the guard. He'll kill me. I can't do it." Then he thought, "You know what? I have to have certainty. The kabbalist wouldn't have put me in this situation if he believed it would bring me harm."

He found the strength and showed the folded piece of paper to the guard, who became very excited. He said, "Oh, my God! I can't believe you're here. Why didn't you let me know you were coming?" He cared for the student and took him to see his family, where the student was able to see his father.

The student came back to the kabbalist and said: "Thank you so much for giving me that note. I don't understand what you did." The kabbalist told him, "You want to know the truth? The truth is I did nothing. I gave you a blank piece of paper. However, because you believed that piece of paper was going to save you, you had certainty. I did nothing. It was all you."

The power is always in our hands, not anybody else's. We might go to a rabbi, priest, or shaman for help. They will support us along our journey, but the decisions, the actions, are up to us. And there is only thing that makes them work: certainty.

[Light-Work]

I want to introduce you to another k-Tool that will assist in bringing out our proactive potential. We have created a 4-step k-Tool known as THE TRANSFORMATION FORMULA. Every time you find yourself facing a challenge, remember these four steps:

1. A challenge or an obstacle occurs. Your reactive nature runs the risk of being triggered.
2. Recognize and realize that your reaction is the real enemy. Your anger, outrage, defensiveness, and blame are the real enemy. The other person or the circumstance is not. They're merely the messenger, there to push your buttons.
3. Stop. Hit that pause button. Take control over the part of you that wants to justify blame. Remember the questions: Why is this happening? Why is this in my movie? What's the deeper meaning? What's really going on here?

4. What can I do to transform this potential challenge and obstacle into an opportunity to reveal light? Take that action.

Here is the **Transformation Formula** in encapsulated form. Copy this, laminate it, and carry it with you.

An obstacle occurs.

My reaction is the real enemy.

Stop, pause, and inject consciousness. What am I doing here? Am I going to feed the black wolf or the white wolf?

Express my proactive nature to transform this challenge into an opportunity to reveal Light.

For your Light-Work, try to incorporate the **Transformation Formula** into your life. Over the next few days, any time you come up against a challenge or obstacle, remember these four steps and see if you can use this formula to assist you in transforming anything uncomfortable and potentially chaotic in your life into an opportunity to reveal Light. Write down what happens. Notice the darkness in your life begin to give way to warmth and light.

Two
Worlds

Chapter 13
Two Worlds

The last Light-Work introduced another k-Tool, known as the **Transformation Formula**. We gave you an opportunity to tackle any obstacle or challenge with the four steps of the formula. As you undoubtedly discovered, it's not easy. Like anything, it requires practice, but rest assured that life will offer you no end of opportunities to practice! Consistently using the formula means saying goodbye to a robotic life of reactivity.

Two Worlds

As we have mentioned before, there is more to life than what you see. Kabbalists explain that there are two worlds that coexist simultaneously in parallel dimensions:

1. <u>The physical world</u>: the world that is dictated by our senses. If we can see it, touch it, smell it, taste it, or hear it, it's in our physical reality. The only problem with the five senses

is that they are limited. For example, you can't see behind you. You can't smell with your hands. And the five senses include our intellect, our ego, and, therefore, our judgments, which makes the physical world a very subjective place.

Kabbalists show us we have to be very careful if we're going to interpret life only with our five senses, because our senses are so limited. It would be like making some of our biggest life decisions (choosing our spouse, buying our dream home, going into business with someone, investing all our money) with only 1 Percent of the information we needed. It's like being blindfolded and hoping that every choice we make somehow turns out okay.

How can we possibly expect to have the results we want in our life if we're guessing at every turn, and going through life like it's a casino? Fortunately, Kabbalah explains that there is another world.

2. <u>The spiritual dimension</u>: the remaining 99 Percent of reality. As I mentioned earlier, scientists look at an atom under a powerful microscope and see that only one percent of that atom is really physical; the remaining 99 percent is void of matter. That 99 Percent reality is the spiritual realm, and it is the domain of the Light. Kabbalists explain that this is where the Light of fulfillment originates.

Our goal in life is to find a way to bring these two dimensions together. Let's face it, we are physical beings and we live in a physical world. We have to eat, sleep, and pay bills. We have to take care of ourselves. We need clothing, shelter—very physical, tangible things. But if we live purely in the 1 Percent reality, we live in the world of illusion. We only see the effects in our life. As we've said, the source of all of those effects is not physical in nature. It's energy, or consciousness. It's the 99 Percent realm.

Seeking Answers

Prayer is one of those mystical tools that most people believe in; they believe we can talk to the Creator, ask for help and, hopefully, affect things in our life. Well, if that's so, why do our prayers sometimes go unanswered? The answer lies in the 99 Percent. The world of the 1 Percent, in Kabbalah, is the world of questions. We question everything. We don't believe in anything. We have to see and feel in order to believe. Our prayers can't be answered in the world of questions. However, if we move ourselves to the world of answers, to the world of the 99 Percent and the world of certainty, our prayers get answered every time.

Bruce Morgan, Ph.D., is the associate director for the Space Telescope Science Institute in Baltimore. He says, "It's a fairly embarrassing situation to admit that we can't find 99 percent of the Universe." This is thousands of years after the *Zohar* talked about the nature of these two worlds. This profound observation by a top contemporary scientist gives further credence to the fact that the world of 99 Percent is not just a theory designed to make us feel good about the limitations of our five senses.

We all have our evidence. We know for sure that our five senses deceive us. How many times have we become enraptured by a relationship with someone, been head-over-heels in love only to find out a few weeks or months later that this person isn't really who we thought they were? Why didn't we see this the first time we met them? Because a lot of those character traits were concealed. The flakiness or anger issues or alcohol problem was hidden from view.

The 1 Percent world is purely the world of illusion—the world of short-term gratification. We only see fulfillment in what we have in front of us. Take caffeine, for example. It will give us a bit of a buzz, and it will give us this buzz immediately. The 1 Percent world is always instantaneous. The problem is that its results don't last. The buzz fades. So the 1 Percent reality is the world of temporary fulfillment, while the 99 Percent reality is the realm of lasting fulfillment, of real Light.

The World of Information

Rav Berg calls the 99 Percent realm the world of information. For every single question we have, the answer exists in the world of the 99 Percent. You meet a new person and wonder, are we compatible? Will we have a relationship? Is there something about this person that I should know that could affect the course of our relationship? The answers do exist—they exist in the world of the 99 percent. If you knew everything about them immediately, you might not even start that relationship, and there would be no opportunity for growth, no opportunity to reveal Light. If my friend had recognized immediately that the woman he was seeing was as deep into her cocaine addiction as she was, would he have ever moved forward? Would he have ever become such a compassionate, effective Drug Counselor?

The truth is that we have complete access to all of the information that we could ever desire—even information about the people we interact with. It's like having the most comprehensive encyclopedia at our fingertips all of the time. We just choose not to open the book. But the clues are always there. Anything in the world of 99 percent is just as possible and just as real as that which exists in the 1 percent realm. The information is always there. We just usually choose not to use it because we are more comfortable with the 1 Percent—what we see and experience with our senses.

The Mystical Realm

We understand that the 99 Percent is a mystical realm of unseen forces. We relate to the 99 Percent with our sixth sense, with our consciousness, which is not physical. Imagine, for example, fertilizing an egg. We understand the physicality of conception: the sperm and the egg come together and a child is conceived. But the idea that from one tiny cell there is an entire replication of DNA elements that creates a human body is quite mind-blowing! It's mystical. Yes, we see a physical manifestation of life, but there is also a Soul, the consciousness that is created between two physical components, that exists in tandem with the physical body. Here the 99 percent and 1 percent realms are intimately united.

In this way we are directly linked to the 99 percent. What is intuition? Where do creative bursts of inspiration come from? These are ways by which we receive information from the non-physical world. There are endless examples of how some of the greatest thinkers of our time tapped into this world. It is said that Mozart could hear his symphonies in seconds. Paul McCartney said he woke up one morning with the lyrics for "Yesterday." The biochemist, Mendeleyev, who was responsible for the Periodic Table of Elements saw the table in a dream he had. All of these individuals were connecting to the 99 Percent realm of consciousness.

You don't have to be a philosopher, musician, chemist, or inventor to have a personal way of relating to the 99 Percent. Have you ever been thinking of a friend you haven't talked to in ten or fifteen years, and as you're thinking of them, they call you? What do we tell ourselves? We say, "What an amazing coincidence!" Or, maybe you're singing a song that you haven't even heard in years. You get in the car, turn on the radio and, boom, there is the song. Is life really so random?

Of course not. These are examples of *synchronicity*—a meaningful convergence of events that is a result of the law of cause and effect. With our limited 1 Percent view, however, we can't see the connection. We think it's by chance, accidental. It's not that the 99 Percent world cannot be tested, but it's not easily detectable at first glance. If we strongly desire a feeling of fulfillment, satisfaction, and approval (all non-physical, 99 percent attributes), we are setting forth a condition in which we might receive a job promotion in the 1 percent world. We might not readily make the connection when we receive the promotion, but the connection between our thoughts and the promotion exists nonetheless.

Our Job

Remember Michelangelo, who illustrated the notion of chipping away at what you don't need? His sculpture of David already existed; he merely removed the excess rock to uncover it. That's what the 99 Percent is. Everything exists in this Universe in the form of potential. There is, in fact, nothing new under the sun; it just hasn't been brought into physical form yet in the 1 Percent realm. Our job is to reveal the 99 Percent, which is another way of saying the Light.

Think of the Internet. The Internet is an interesting metaphor because the Internet is not something you can touch or hold. It's not physical. You can't put the Internet in your drawer. There might be physical cables and computer screens that give us access to the Internet, but it's not tangible in itself. Yet it can provide us with all sorts of physical goodies. We can order a pizza and have it delivered. We can buy a house or meet our soul mate. But we have to connect to it through an interface in order to physically manifest what we want in our here and now. The Internet, like the 99 percent realm, represents the potential for all things physical.

We could also say that the 99 Percent is the realm of miracles, but it's important to understand that a miracle does not occur in the 99 Percent realm; it takes place in the 1 Percent world. The source of that miracle may come from the 99 Percent, but it has to manifest in our physical world. We must have evidence of it before it can be called a miracle. If we don't see its effects, it's just potential.

I *could* be the most amazing father, but until I have manifested a child, I'm all talk—all potential. Until we manifest our success (money in the bank, soul mates, houses, health, miraculous cures), until we have physical evidence, we're simply talking about the world of potential. Our job in Kabbalah is to access the 99 Percent source of wisdom, miracles, creativity, imagination, intuition, and fulfillment, and manifest it in the physical world of the 1 Percent reality.

Limitations & Assumptions

We are limited in this 1 Percent world by our five senses, but we're unlimited in the 99 Percent world. We don't have eyes in the back of our head, so we know that our vision is limited. Nor can we smell pizza baking from 100 miles away. With our limited senses, we can't experience the big picture.

When we can see the big picture—the 99 Percent reality—we know what our options are. But if we only have 1 Percent of the information, we are destined to remain stuck. We're a victim, the effect.

It's like a riddle. Sometimes a riddle can have the most logical answer, yet we fail to see it because of how our mind filters information. For example, a father and his son are in an accident.

They take the son to the Emergency Room and then send him to surgery. The doctor looks at the patient and says: "Oh my God, this is my son!" Who is the doctor? At first, you might find yourself scratching your head. But what if I told you that the answer is the boy's mother? That makes perfect sense. Why didn't we think of that? Our filter told us that it couldn't be the mother, before we even had a second to correct our assumption that the doctor was male. I love riddles like this one. One second, you don't have the answer; the next second you do. The information seems to appear suddenly. That's the 99 Percent at work—solutions to problems and answers to riddles appear instantaneously when we are open to receiving them.

We make assumptions and judgments about people all the time, based upon their appearance, what car they drive, where they live, how much money they have. Then, of course, we compare ourselves to that person. We tell ourselves, if I don't have that car, I don't measure up. We're stuck, based upon our 1 Percent illusion of what we believe is successful. We see successful people or celebrities in the media all of the time, and we have all sorts of beliefs about this person's inner world, life, marriage, family, and values. We might put them on a pedestal, but unbeknownst to us, they may have a problem with drugs or relationships. Assumptions are interpretations based on our own ego, experiences, memories, and projections, and it's a strong possibility that our assumptions are way offbase.

Our false assumptions lead us to practice all sorts of self-destructive behaviors in an attempt to look and be like those we idolize. Plastic surgery. Eating disorders. We get sucked into the 1

Percent world of what people look like on the outside without full knowledge of the pain and lack of fulfillment that might exist on the inside. The physical world simply cannot provide us with the whole story.

Synchronicity

We want answers and are starting to recognize the limitations of the 1 Percent. We recognize that money doesn't necessarily bring happiness. We know, based upon our life's experiences, that it's not enough just to have physical stuff. After all, as the saying goes: we "can't take it with us." We don't come to this physical world to accomplish physical things. We come here to make a spiritual correction.

People today are more open to the 99 Percent, especially as it relates to health. Acupuncture, homeopathy, and other health fields rooted in the 99 percent realm are increasing in popularity. Western medicine is based very much in the 1 Percent, and many people are beginning to recognize the limitations of viewing health completely through this lens. Medicine that is rooted in the 1 Percent has its successes and can play an important role, but it can be far more effective when we also tap into the limitless wisdom and answers that exist in the 99 percent.

When you're connected to the 99 percent, you are "in the zone." When athletes go to that place where every move they make is perfectly orchestrated, they're tapping into the 99 Percent. Hockey player Mark Messier, in the 1994 Stanley Cup playoffs, entered this space. Magic Johnson said he felt like basketball games slowed down for him; he, too, often tuned in to the 99 Percent. Whether you're playing hockey and you can't stop scoring goals against your Opponent, or you're a basketball player and the game moves in slow motion, or you're a tennis player who seems to be everywhere on the court at once—you're in the zone—you're tapping in to the 99 percent and letting go of beliefs that limit us, that shut us down.

Occasionally we find ourselves in the zone, and it feels great. But most of the time, we find ourselves under the spell of the 1 Percent. Do you remember the Boston Red Sox and the "the curse of the Bambino?" For almost a century, the Red Sox couldn't win the World Series, until 2004 when they finally triumphed over the New York Yankees to win the title. After decades of limiting beliefs and operating in the 1 percent, the team finally connected to their true limitless potential. And once they believed, they did it again in 2007.

Sometimes the information we receive from the 99 percent surprises us. We have absolutely no idea how we tapped into it or where it came from. Once I went to a concert with a friend of mine to see the band Chicago. In the middle of the concert, we went to get a drink. I said, " What happened when you were nine?" He was shocked by the sudden question and said: "I never told this to anyone, I was abused when I was nine." Until the moment the insight came to me, I was completely unaware of this part of my friend's past. I simply felt that something had happened when he was nine years old.

I know I am not the only one who has had an experience like this. We have all had sensations or "funny feelings" about people or situations. Many times we discount these feelings because we feel unsure of ourselves, our innate wisdom, and the power of the 99 Percent, but as we continue our work, our trust will grow.

[Light-Work]

In order to see the contrast between these two worlds—the 1 Percent and the 99 Percent—let's take a little test. Look at the following sentence, read it to yourself and count how many letter F's you see. You have ten seconds. Go.

Finished files are the result of years of scientific study combined with the experience of years.

Okay, time's up. How many F's did you count? Did you see three? Four? Five? Or did you get the correct number—six?

Shocking, right? How is it that every time I've given this test to a group of students, there has never been a unanimous decision on how many F's there are? You'll notice that as you're reading this sentence, three of the F's sounds like a V. We miss it. Right? One of the limitations of our five senses is that we're patterned to hear a V instead of an F, so we don't see what's in front of us. There are no tricks. Everyone is looking at exactly the same sentence.

What's the lesson? We cannot trust our limited five senses.

Over the next week or two, start to let go of the limitations of your five senses in the 1 Percent world and start to connect more with the unlimited 99 Percent world. We all have the ability. Trust your intuition. Look for signs over these next few days. Pay particular attention to synchronicities or coincidences, intuition, creative inspiration, miracles. Note any signs you see in your journal. All we need is desire and awareness in order to connect with the 99 Percent.

Chapter 14
Power of the 99 Percent

Your Light-Work was to look for signs, messages, and synchronous events—evidence of the existence of the 99 percent. Did you notice anything? Did you have sparks of inspiration that seemed to come from "nowhere?" Fine tuning this skill takes time. But once you begin to notice your connection to the 99 percent in small ways, you'll soon start to notice bigger examples of this unseen world.

Patterns of Energy

We talk about spirituality all the time, but what does it really mean? In the movie *What the Bleep Do We Know?* there is a demonstration by a famous researcher from Japan named Dr. Masaru Emoto. In his experiments, he played different kinds of music near several bottles of water. Twenty-four hours later he looked at the molecular structure of the water in those bottles. He discovered that the soothing and relaxing Baroque music of

Mozart created orderly, beautiful, molecular patterns. When he played other kinds of music, loud, distorted guitars and heavy metal, the structure of the water was very chaotic and messy.

That led him to his next experiment, which was writing different messages on the bottles of water. If Dr. Emoto wrote messages of joy, love, and happiness, the next day the molecular structure of the water was similar to that of a beautiful snowflake. On the other hand, if a bottle had written on it, "You make me sick," the water molecules formed disjointed patterns.

What can we infer from this experiment? That sound and thought are powerful vibrations of energy that create changes in our physical environment. When thoughts of love and joy are expressed, the physical world changes to reflect these positive vibrations. When thoughts of hatred, darkness, and negativity prevail, the physical world also changes to reflect these negative forces. So, the law of cause and effect can either work for us, or it can create chaos.

The beauty of this particular movie is that it indicates that people are becoming open to these kinds of insights. Quantum physics isn't new. Kabbalah has been talking about quantum consciousness for thousands of years, and now those who have the desire are being given the opportunity to see the principles at work in a bottle of water—and in their lives.

Healing

I took my mom and dad to Houston awhile back to see the doctors about 18 months after my father's stroke. He went through a series of MRIs and other tests so we could figure out how to take him to the next level of recovery. One doctor looked at the scan and asked: "Could you bring me the right scan? The person with this scan shouldn't be able to walk or talk." It *was* the right scan. More than half of my father's brain was dead; there was no activity in the parts of his brain that control conversation. The reactive part of the brain worked, but the initiator component of his brain was dead. Physical movement of any kind shouldn't have been possible. The doctors told us that it was a miracle that a person with such decreased brain activity could actually walk and talk.

This tells us that my father found the ability to use the parts of his brain that were living to do the job of the cells that were dead. The Rav had ignored the doctors who said that this or that would be impossible; he just went about his business of creating his inner healing with absolute certainty. It was as if he wanted to show the world what we can all do. All of us should have the capacity to take control over the functioning of the body, because, after all, it's all consciousness.

In Malcolm Gladwell's book *Blink*, there is an interesting reference to Warren Buffet, saying that sometimes he would know that there was a shift happening in the stock market because he would get a backache. Recognizing that your backache is connected to the stock market is not 1 Percent living; that's 99 Percent living. Everyone has the ability to receive information from the 99 percent realm, not just Warren Buffet. What signs have you noticed lately that you have been downplaying?

How the Universe Shows Up & How We Interpret It

A woman, a student of Kabbalah, was in an addictive, long-distance relationship with a man in New York. He was emotionally unavailable, a little abusive, and showed no respect for her at all. This had gone on for five years by the time she met with me. Here's a classic example of a very smart, savvy, intellectual woman who made a poor choice and was finally trying to break away. She recognized the need to end this relationship, but she'd been invited to a big gala event in New York. She asked me, "Should I go to New York? It's very tempting, because I know he's going to be there. But I know it is time to break away. What should I do?"

I said, "Well, you have a choice. You can go to the event and potentially run into this guy and get addicted all over again. Or you can choose not to go. Why don't you ask the Light for a message? Tap into the 99 Percent to get some clarity." She came back on Monday morning with a big smile on her face and said: "I got my message. I was driving in Hollywood up Vine Boulevard, thinking, 'What should I do?' I looked up and saw this huge billboard that said, *Come to New York*. It was such an obvious test coming from the Opponent, because I knew it was exactly what I wanted to hear. I wanted the drama. I wanted to get pulled into my addiction again and to feel the temporary satisfaction that comes from being with him. But I knew the Light was trying to say, 'Listen, you want to go with your five senses and get some instant gratification? Sure, go have a fun weekend and then be devastated for months.' I chose to trust what the Light was telling me, which was to go against my addictive nature." I was really happy for her because she got it. It could have been a sign that said: *Don't Go to New York to Continue Your Abusive Relationship.* But she understood the subtle way in which the Light was sending her the message.

There is a story about the ways in which the Light communicates with us. There was a very religious guy who'd been living in a house for years when a terrible storm hit and his house began to flood, but he refused to be evacuated. He stood on his porch and said: "I've been here forty years. God loves me. And God will take care of me."

People were fleeing town as the flood water got higher and higher. The Coast Guard came along and threw out a life preserver to the man, but he said: "No, I know that God is going to save me." The waters got higher still, and another boat came along. The man still insisted God was going to save him. Finally the water completely submerged the house and he was holding on to the chimney. A helicopter threw down a rope but he stubbornly refused. "No, God is going to save me."

As a result, the guy drowned. He reached the gates of heaven and said to God: "In all these years, I've stood firm. I believed in you. I always said you would save me. And the one time I really needed you, you abandoned me."

And God replied, "I didn't abandon you. I sent you the Coast Guard, a boat, and a helicopter." Like this man, we often don't see the messages that are right in front of our eyes. We don't hear what we need to hear, because we get stubborn, closed, and locked into the world of the 1 Percent. But there is another way. When we allow ourselves to crush our egos, to ask for help from the Light, and to look for signs and messages, there is a connection available that can completely change our limited perspective.

If we look at our lives, there are billions of little stories—small but powerful moments day after day that brought us to the place we are presently at. Had different choices been made, alternative routes taken, we would be in a completely different place. You can tell where you have been living—in the world of the 99 percent or the world of the 1 percent—by your current circumstances. If you have been completely in the 1 Percent, you are suffering to the fullest extent possible. On the other hand, living solely in the 99 Percent means you are experiencing the absolute best outcome possible—a life filled with immeasurable joy and immense fulfillment.

There is a great story of one of our students, who had just gone through a terrible divorce and her ex-husband had ruined their credit. She was trying to buy a house and start her life over, but she couldn't get a bank loan. She was devastated and feeling as much chaos as one person can feel. She was trying to break out of victim mode, trying to let go, but it was very difficult for her to move on. She'd been cheated on, dumped, and she was upset. She felt stuck, blocked. We had a conversation about connecting to the 99 Percent, the big picture, where miracles can happen if we get out of our way.

It was Saturday night and she was at home feeling pretty sorry for herself. A friend called and said: "Hey, we're having a small dinner party. We'd love you to come over."

She didn't hesitate , "No, I'm depressed and I'd just be a burden."

Her friend insisted, "There are fun people here. Just come and hang out with us."

She remembered our conversation and saw that the simple thing to do was to stay home, be miserable, and justify herself as a victim. But, she thought, "Obviously, I'm missing the big picture here. Maybe it will be good for me to go. Maybe I'll meet some new friends."

She went to the dinner party and tried to put on a happy face. She ended up sitting next to a man who, it turned out, ran a bank. By the end of the night, he had arranged a loan for her to buy a house. This is not a relationship story. I am not talking soul mates here. It was even better than that at this time in her life; she sat next to the one guy in town who could say: "Don't worry about your credit. I'll give you the loan." This woman started her life over by getting out of her own way and trusting that, although she didn't feel like going to a party, she didn't always see what was best. She knew that if we let go and ask for help, the Light will always guide us. The banker didn't come knocking on her door, but because she was willing to get out of her own way, she allowed a miracle to happen. To this day, this woman is a changed person because of that one decision she made—the decision to let the 99 Percent guide her to become a better version of herself than she ever thought possible.

Life is like a series of parallel Universes, like a shelf full of movies lined up along the wall at Blockbuster. You want to make sure you're choosing the movie that will bring you the most enjoyment, passion, and excitement. You want a movie with the best people and the most awesome cinematography. In order to find this movie, we have to be willing to do our homework, so we don't get stuck in our old feelings, moods, and opinions. Only when we clear the debris, can we tap into the guidance of the 99 Percent.

Miracles

Miracles are considered a technology in Kabbalah. A miracle is not something extraordinary, a phenomenon that falls out of the sky. It's not some random event; quite the opposite, a miracle is the ultimate manifestation of cause and effect. It's a tool.

Where do miracles originate? In the 99 Percent realm. But they manifest in the 1 Percent, in the physical world. A medical miracle shows up on a test or an MRI. A financial miracle, like the woman who needed a bank loan to buy a house, manifests as money in her bank account. For a woman who is trying to get pregnant but can't conceive, the miracle would be her becoming pregnant and having a baby. Miracles are mind over matter—the consciousness of the 99 Percent outweighing the power of the 1 Percent world.

It all leads back to one of the first things we discussed in this book: what do we really want? Do we want instant gratification? Do we want the house, the boat, the car? Or do we want to get the most out of this life? If we're on a path that's reactive and egotistical, we may get instant gratification, but in the end, it leads to chaos. If we want to live as the best possible version of ourselves, it will take a little more work. But it's all a question of what we want. Now that we understand more, it's time to go back to that first question and review the answers we wrote down when we began our work. Would your answers be the same now? Hopefully, you have grown in your perspective and your values during the course of this book, and your new answers reflect this growth. After all, this is a book on *Living Kabbalah*. It's about transformation. No more sticking our heads in the sands of denial. We know too much now.

The 99 Percent realm has the ability to change our physical reality through our thoughts, intentions, and focus. We can go from having no money to creating abundance; we can choose to have quality relationships where we were once isolated and lonely. We can have physical health instead of the illness and disease that plagued our body before. Our job is to connect to that potential through consciousness, change our nature, and then bring the miracles into manifestation.

The following Light-Work exercise speaks to this specifically.

Think about some particular aspect of your life where you really need clarity. Do you have a question about whether you should proceed in a relationship, or whether you should end it? Are you wondering if you should change your business, your career? Go back to school? Whatever it might be, commit your question to writing. Our mission is to get clarity on this issue from the 99 Percent realm, uncorrupted by intellect, opinion, and memories.

Spend a few days listening for that answer, looking for signs, because you will be guided. Remember, a light doesn't go on in a darkened room, unless there is a desire in the person to turn it on by flipping the light switch. In the same way, when we ask for clarity from the 99 Percent, the law of cause and effect tells us we will always get our answer. We just need to actively listen.

Make a log of any answers that you receive from the 99 Percent. It may not be easy at first to distinguish between what your ego is saying and what the 99 Percent is trying to communicate to you, so note all of it. Gradually, we'll start to discern the source of that information.

This is a lot of fun—a real adventure! Notice how excited you are at the prospect of getting clarity without bias, just 100% pure Light. The Light sees past limitations, and knows exactly what you need to ensure the most optimal and fulfilling Universe for yourself.

Corrections & Consciousness

Chapter 15

Your Garbage, Your Gift

Imagine that you have an important meeting to drive to at nine A.M., but it's rush hour and it's raining. You jump in the car, giving yourself enough time to get to your destination, allowing for the traffic and weather conditions. Down the street, one of your neighbors is pulled over and the hood of his car is open. Now you've got a moral dilemma. You're in a hurry. You need to get to this meeting. But you know this person. Do you keep driving and hope he doesn't see you? Or do you take the time to pull over to see if there is anything you can do to help?

Let's say you go the extra mile and pull over to help. It turns out that the battery is dead, and his car needs a jump start. You have cables in your car. But it's raining, miserable outside, and you're cutting it close with the time. What do you do? Like any good neighbor who wants do the proactive thing, you decide to take the extra few minutes to help and hope it all works out.

Of course, if you're going to help someone to jumpstart a car, first you have to lift up the hood of your own car and start connecting to the batteries. Well, when was the last time you looked under your hood? It's greasy and messy in there. Dead leaves and insects, grease and grime—it's not pretty. And it's not convenient. At this point, are you willing to roll up your sleeves and get messy? The lesson is that in order for us to help another person, and get to a place where we are really sharing, we must be willing to deal with a little filth—namely, our own.

This chapter introduces the idea of being willing to get under our own hood, to take a look at our own garbage–even when it's inconvenient. Remember what Michelangelo taught us about his sculpture of David? When we chip away at rock, we find the perfection that lies underneath.

Garbage Hides

Where is the Light hiding when we find ourselves in a mess of our own making? The truth is that we're in a spiritual game of Hide and Seek. Our Light hides under our garbage, behind our ego, and underneath our anger and depression. The more of our garbage we unearth, the more Light we reveal. This is the kabbalistic concept of personal correction, called *Tikkun* in Aramaic. It means that we can repair and correct any aspect of ourselves, our personality, or our behavior that is reactive, selfish, blocked. We can turn our trash into treasures.

We do a good job of hiding our garbage. We try to show the world how perfect we are, how unblemished we are, putting our best foot forward at all times. So the first step is recognition. In order to start recognizing our garbage, we need to realize that our Universe is a big mirror. We look at our world, our friends, our family, and ask, what happens that triggers us? What do we see in others? The answer: we see ourselves. The traits that bother us in others are the same traits that we don't like in ourselves. The whole Universe is there to show us our garbage.

Actually I think it's more of a magnifying glass than a mirror. If you put a magnifying glass over a leaf, you can direct the heat and intensity of the sun, setting the leaf on fire. This is very exciting when you're a kid, although your parents might have a different opinion. The same effect takes place when we are set ablaze with mirror images of our own defects of character. But human beings have a way of deferring the heat; it's called denial. We have a defense mechanism that says: *"I can't handle this. It's too much!"* In Kabbalah, denial is what occurs in the presence of direct Light, when there is such intense Light illuminating us that we shut down. As the saying goes: "If you can't take the heat, you better get out of the kitchen." But what do you do when the kitchen is your life?

Where do we hide when it's too hot, or there is too much sun? We find the shade. And the shade is just another way of saying a blockage. This idea comes from Carl Jung, by the way. Jung studied Kabbalah and came up with the notion of the shadow. We don't have to know anything about Jungian analysis to under-stand his concept: if we put something between us and light, we create a shadow. If we put something between us and the Light, we're creating a blockage. We're preventing ourselves from receiving Light and from sharing Light. That's what Jung meant: we all have a shaded side. We all have garbage and blockages.

Our Light hides behind our darkness, not behind what we're good at. Say you're born with ADD, like I was. You can hide behind it, take some pills, and be less than you were intended to be. Or you can use the condition to better yourself. Because my brain can't relax, I involve myself in many different projects so I don't lose focus. I have found a way to transform my garbage into a gift.

We don't become the person we were intended to become through the things that we're naturally good at. A person who does something truly extraordinary is someone who is transforming his or her garbage into Light, because our garbage is really the gift we give to the world. Transformation is our life's work. In other words, our mission is to find the coal and create the diamond. It's not an easy process. It's not something that we necessarily enjoy. But it's something that we must do to obtain ultimate fulfillment.

How do we know what our garbage is?

How do we know what we're here to correct? Sometimes it's obvious. If someone is constantly angry, raging, or abusive, I think it's pretty obvious what the garbage is. But not everyone is so obviously a mess. We may be functioning very well. We may be very successful, happily married, a good parent, and we're simply looking for spiritual meaning and some answers. It's not that our life is garbage. This is a very important distinction. We're talking about *aspects* of our lives, repetitive patterns that cause us to feel stuck or limited. And it's not always in-your-face stuff. Very successful, highly functioning people can also benefit enormously from the excavation process that leads to transformation.

So what about a person with a big heart who cares a great deal about other people? Why is that person in the physical world? We all have something to transform. We mentioned the Libran complex, the idea that a person can be an incredibly kind and thoughtful person, yet have a difficult time setting limits and letting go of what others think of them. Our garbage might be concealed in similar ways. It's not always sitting out there on the front lawn.

We all have garbage. We all have blind spots, those patterns that keep us from growing, but they're not always obvious to others or to us. One of the things that we might do if we're not sure what it is we're here to fix is to ask. Remember that extra credit exercise about asking a friend, someone close to us, to tell us what we needed to fix? It's not too late to ask this question. If you are apprehensive, just ask your friend casually: *Do you see a pattern in me where I repeatedly tend to get in my own way?*

In this work, we have to be willing to look for what we cannot see easily–the hidden aspects of our ego, the seed level, the buried and concealed garbage. In psychology we learn about a tool called the *Johari Window*, named after its inventors Joseph Luft and Harry Ingham. The aspects of the *Johari Window* include:

- Those things that we know about our self and that are known to others (open).

- Those things that we know about our self and that are not known to others (hidden).

- Those things that we don't know about our self and that are known to others (blind).

- Those things that we don't know about our self and that are not known by others (unknown).

Right now we may be blind to our garbage, but at least we are aware that, unless we're saints, we have some. That's the first step. Next we identify our core issues, admit that we see our garbage.

Getting Our Buttons Pushed

How many of us get irritated by other people's actions? One of the things that bothers a good friend of mine is when he has to listen to someone tell a story that he's heard at least five times already. Of course, my friend wants to be polite. But sometimes he'll say: "You've told this story ten times. That bugs me. Don't you remember when you told me the same story two days ago?" Sometimes my friend's judging nature can create distance in relationships.

What are the things that irritate us in other people's actions and behaviors? Are we annoyed when our friends are always late? We may find it disrespectful, but they don't get it, and we can't believe they don't get it. Are we offended when people are rude, curt, or abrasive? Or when people take too long to tell us something? Why are they wasting our time? Personally, I can't also deal with meetings that last more than fifteen minutes. I totally check out.

I know someone who moved to California more than twenty years ago from an English boarding school background, and he couldn't believe how unreliable and flaky people are in L.A. How can people say things that they don't mean, not follow through, not keep their word? He was frustrated for years until he realized it was cultural.

One of the principles that Kabbalah teaches us is that it's important that our buttons get pushed. Not only is it okay, but it's necessary for growth. Every time a button gets pushed, it forces us to pay close attention to an aspect of our reactivity that needs an adjustment. Whether it is our mother-in-law, our spouse, or our coworkers who drive us mad, others push our buttons in order for us to realize what it is in us that we need to change. The Universe is working in collaboration with us so that we can transform our garbage and move to the next level, out of darkness. If this process didn't occur, we'd be living in a fantasy in which everything was perfectly arranged and flowing beautifully. But if that were the case, then why did we come into this physical world? You know the answer by now: there has to be something we're here to repair, or we wouldn't be here.

Digging Through Our Garbage

Having our buttons pushed is one way to discover those traits that we need to correct. The other way that we can get a glimpse of our garbage is by looking for repetitive patterns that limit or block us. It's like the movie "Groundhog Day," in which the same scenario occurs day after day after day. It's the same chaos, the same fall down the same pit. Bill Murray's character keeps tripping over the same sidewalk, stepping in the same puddle—until he has a change in consciousness. At the end of the movie, when he finally sees life differently, things start to line up in synchrony to allow his life to change.

We all have habits and patterns, and we need to recognize them as such, or we will never change. This is step two: look for patterns in your life that do not bring you joy. Do you tend to have the same type of dead-end relationships? Do you have a pattern of pushing people away? One major pattern is choosing someone who is emotionally unavailable. When you counsel hundreds of people consistently over decades, as I have, you start to see there's something in these patterns.

Like self sabotage.

What will always be true of people with victim consciousness? They will always make sure that they sabotage themselves over and over again. If they're starting to become successful in some area of life, they will shoot themselves in the foot to avoid the future possibility of disappointment. They'll sabotage a relationship by cheating on the person or by convincing the other person that they don't deserve them. They'll push them away. They'll sabotage a job opportunity by blowing the deal, or by not showing up at work, or by being flaky. The technique changes but the underlying pattern is still the same.

Self-sabotage insures we can't get ahead. Thinking small guarantees we'll never get to the next level. Picking an unavailable person will mean we will never have fulfillment in the relationship, because the person can't give us what we're looking for. There is a great quote from Helen Keller about life being a succession of lessons that must be lived to be understood. It's amazing how we think that we're all pretty smart, savvy, accomplished people. Yet, it's not until we go through an experience or crisis that emotionally devastates us that we start to see our patterns. Few people choose a spiritual path or engage in self-help when everything is going beautifully.

Of course, we might also see the pattern and choose to ignore it. It's not enough to recognize patterns; we also have to be willing to get to the core. What causes our garbage? How can we prevent more accumulation?

It's impossible after merely a week, or even a few months of studying Kabbalah to get to our core issues. We're dealing with an onion. There are many layers to peel away before getting to the core; it takes time and effort. But if we're constantly giving in to our patterns, if we're constantly judging others instead of looking at our own negative qualities, we'll keep feeding the ego. It will be much harder to find our core issues while we're living our patterns and letting the judgment of others rule our thoughts.

It's important to know that there is a time when the same trigger that may have upset us for years no longer creates the same response. People will always gossip or be negative. They will always complain. But there comes a time when we have such resilience and certainty in who we are and what we're doing, that when these people come along, their behavior rolls off us like water on a duck's back. It doesn't affect us the same way. They haven't changed, but our response has.

The lesson is that these core challenges will come up again and again until we have corrected them in our consciousness. We won't have the same responses to our triggers forever. If someone has a fear of flying, for example, once they've conquered that fear—with effort and discipline—they can fly with no problem.

A student once asked me: "Is it worth all of this effort to change myself? I do all this work and then, maybe fifty years from now, on my death bed, I'll get the fulfillment."

He was overlooking an important point. The process *is* the fulfillment.

It's not about waiting fifty years and getting our reward. As we are removing layers, we are revealing more and more Light. As we're peeling the layers, we're getting closer to the core. We're getting to the fruit, the sweetness. The relief and fulfillment happen as we strip away the layers.

When we're looking to find our core issue, even before we find it we experience the fulfillment that comes with the process. As we move towards the Light, the Light moves towards us. But if we're on a path of reactivity and ego, even if we don't deserve that darkness, it's going to come to us because we're on a path that's leading us in that direction. Start on the path towards the Light. The Light will meet you there, even before you reach your destination.

[Light-Work]

Here's something fun to do if you go to a party and don't know anybody. First, take out the garbage. Go around and collect any garbage that people might have, like a crumpled napkin or empty plates and cups. Pretty soon, people will want to meet the busy garbage guy.

We're all working on becoming busy garbage collectors through our study and Light-Work. Our work requires that we dive head first into the dumpster. We have to be willing to get in there, sort through the garbage, and see what we can reclaim and what we need to leave behind. We're not going to find our core issues right away—that's the nature of garbage. Concealed behind the garbage, behind the ego, behind the chaos, is Light waiting to be revealed.

Answer the follow questions in your journal:

1. *How does my garbage show up?*
   What are my traits? Where do I need to make my correction? Am I lazy? Do I procrastinate? How do I get annoyed?

Do I have a temper? When I get stressed out, am I impatient? Am I judgmental, critical?

2. *What is it that bothers me about others?*
   What is it that triggers or pushes my buttons? Is it when people let me down or disappoint me? Is it when people are rude, abrasive, and inconsiderate? Is it when my friends or relatives constantly yell or argue? Identify your own buttons. These are qualities that you don't like about yourself.

3. *What are the ways in which I'm getting stuck in my*
   1 Percent reality, my five senses, my intellect, my ego?
   These might be patterns in your life or habits that you practice, which prevent you from experiencing joy and fulfillment. Write them down in your journal.

Why do we go to a doctor? We have symptoms, right? If we don't know what the symptoms are, we don't know whether or not we're sick. If we don't know what a healthy temperature should be: we don't know if we have a fever. If we don't know what healthy skin looks like: we don't know when we have a rash. In the same way, we need to know what our internal garbage is like so we can sort through it to find the biggest pieces, and transform these into gifts to share with the world.

Chapter 16
Getting to Your Core Issue

Now that you have done your Light-Work and are beginning to see how your garbage shows up in your life, these questions beg to be answered: What do we need to do to remove it permanently? How do we begin to turn these negative traits into gold? We know we have to go to the root of the problem and pull the weed out from there; otherwise, it's just going to keep coming back again, again and again.

Stepping Outside of Ourselves

What is transformation? What can we do to change our inner nature?

In a well-known Kabbalah story that speaks to this idea a man comes to the kabbalist and says his son is sick and the doctors can't help. "Please," he begs the kabbalist, "Do something."

The kabbalist goes into his room, meditates, and does everything he can to tap into the 99 Percent. He comes out and says: "I'm sorry, there is nothing I can do." The man pleads again for his intervention, and finally leaves with a heavy heart. The kabbalist calls his assistant and says: "Gather the ten biggest thieves in the town. Bring them to me." The assistant doesn't ask questions. He gathers the ten thieves, brings them to the kabbalist's house. The kabbalist says, "Take them into my study." The assistant is shocked: no visitors are allowed into the kabbalist's study. Why is he taking these people in there? But he doesn't ask questions.

The kabbalist joins the ten thieves in his study and says: "Let's meditate for this child for one minute." They sit down, meditate on healing for one minute. It's done. They go home.

An hour later, there is a knock on the kabbalist's door, and it's the man with his child. He says, "It's an unbelievable miracle. Ten minutes ago, my child woke up as if there was nothing wrong. Thank you so much. Whatever you did saved my child's life." The man goes home happy.

The assistant, however, is filled with questions. He says, "Master, I don't understand. First the gates were closed. Then, you joined with the thieves, prayed with them, and the gates opened. Why did you bring these criminals into your study? Couldn't you have gathered ten better people—righteous people?"

The kabbalist says, "You're missing the whole point. The gates of heaven were locked, and these thieves knew how to pick a lock."

The real meaning of the story is that a transformative act, in which we go totally against our nature, has tremendous power. Ten righteous people performing a righteous act is to be expected. Ten selfish thieves, who meditate on the healing of somebody else even for one minute, will shatter the gates of heaven.

When we reach a point when someone who has annoyed us our whole life suddenly doesn't trigger us any longer, transformation has occurred. When we make a correction, we're getting closer to our core issue, and we begin to change our destiny.

That's exactly what this story shares. It only took a minute of time for the most self-seeking people to cure a child, because it was such a monumental shift in the thieves' nature. There are plenty of sweet, thoughtful people in this world who are thinking all day long of others, but that doesn't necessarily involve transformation. Core issues have to do with our nature. And, we're talking about changing our nature.

My good friend is a relatively shy, introspective, quiet young lady. She was the kind of kid that her parent's friends would ask: "Does she ever speak?" She had two very outspoken sisters and a very social family, but she was the quiet one. She didn't want to come out of her shell because she was afraid of being rejected and of not being liked. She didn't want to take the risk. When she was in her early twenties, she became a sales person. You can't be a silent sales person and accomplish anything, so she had to learn to speak up. She discovered that her introverted nature was actually a form of ego, as we discussed earlier. For her, the big change was being willing to risk sounding like an idiot some-times. Now she is a sales manager and trains hundreds of new sales people a year—a transformation for someone who used to be so private. For her it has been very freeing to align herself with her real potential and to be able to share her gifts with others.

I, too, understand trepidation around public speaking. I have been around Kabbalah my whole life, but that didn't make public speaking feel any less of a risk to me. I was convinced that no one cared about what I had to say. It was a big stretch for me to stand in front of others and feel comfortable. It's still a challenge for me to completely give of myself to a group of people, although I have no problem giving myself to one person. One of the ways I calm my fear of speaking in front of others is by talking about my own challenges. I make myself talk about me and how I overcome my issues. It's a win-win situation. It makes for a more personal and compelling lecture because I am allowing myself to be real, and it also helps other people open up and share their own issues.

When I get up in front of people and allow myself to be vulnera-ble, I really feel like I am connecting to people. I'm giving them something that will hopefully allow them to explore their own fears and weaknesses. It's important for us to come to a place where we feel strong enough to be weak. The weaker we can become, the more we can share and allow others to share with us, and the closer we can get to our core issues. As long as we have a shell around us, we'll remain separate from the Creator, from uncondi-tional love, and from fulfillment. The protective barriers have to come down, before we can make any spiritual headway.

My friend the sales manager told me about the integrity required for doing her work: returning phone calls, putting out fires, guiding people, and addressing their needs. Early in her exposure to the wisdom of Kabbalah, her teacher asked if she realized that she had a correction to make with every one of her clients. On a spiritual level, for everyone who came into her office, there was something that she had to help this person's Soul to do. This bit of wisdom made my friend realize how she'd been only superficially present for her clients, even though she had helped a lot of people.

When you bare your Soul to someone and let them see your own weaknesses—your failed marriage, troubled relationships, financial fears, or low self-esteem—you offer a real connection and a chance for the other person also to feel understood. It's not an easy thing to do. But by becoming vulnerable and letting people in, we are actually stepping outside of ourselves and connecting to the Light of the Creator.

Veil Exercise

This is a very powerful exercise in a class setting. I ask for a volunteer to come up in front of the whole class, someone who really doesn't want to do this but is willing to trust me. Now this person is sitting in a chair in front of fifty, sixty, or seventy people. It's very scary. The first thing I have her do is look in the eyes of all the students. There is nothing more terrifying than having people see you under that magnifying glass. Then I have her share with us, if she will, what her fears are. Where does she get stuck? What is she afraid of? Amazingly, the person will open up and share.

As she's talking and describing her fear—maybe she has a fear of intimacy or she's afraid that she's not good enough—I will literally place a piece of sheer material that she can still see through over her head. This veil represents a shell, which kabbalists call *klippot*, which keeps us covered up. This veil represents blockage. She continues to talk more deeply about her fears. As she brings up another area in her life where she feels stuck, how much pain it causes her, and how isolated she feels, I place another veil over her head.

I'll ask, "What do you notice now?" She'll say, "Well, you know, I can still see through. There is still light in the room, but I can't make out people's faces anymore. I can't see their eyes. I just see silhouettes." As we start to cover ourselves up and block the Light, the Light is still there, but we miss the details. One of the things that she'll share—as will every person, every time we do this exercise—is that as I place more and more of these veils over her, she feels more comfortable.

It's an amazing phenomenon. As we're describing more and more garbage, more and more ways that we're stuck—our fears that we're alone, that we're no good, that we're awful people, that we'll never amount to anything—as we're describing very personal secrets about ourselves, the physical illusion that people can't see us allows us to feel safer on some level. It's the classic example of the ostrich with his head in the sand who believes if he can't see you, you can't see him. We think that we can't be seen. By the time I've added four, five or six of these veils, the person is sitting in the dark. You could take fifty people out of the room and the person would have no idea they were gone! Although this person is sitting in front of fifty people, he or she feels alone; that's what our fears, our garbage, our core issues of separation create—the illusion that, on one hand, we're comfortable, because people can't see who we really are, and, on the other hand, we're totally disconnected from the people around us.

Finally, the person under the all the veils is crying as she realizes how cut off she is, how alone she is, how isolated and miserable she feels, how she's keeping all this concealed and no one knows. Then I ask her to start talking about what is working in her life, what is meaningful. As she talks about her best friend or maybe her husband's love or her kid smiling at her, I start to lift the veils off her head. Finally there is one last veil sitting over the person's head. So here we are at our last barrier, the last blockage that we need to remove. How do we remove it? Sometimes the person sits there for five minutes until she realizes she needs to take it off herself, because I've stopped taking the veils off.

It's such a metaphor for all of us that we are the ones to remove that last veil. How do we do it? By being willing to come out of the darkness, admitting to our garbage, despite the fact that hiding out feels safe and comfortable. We have to recognize that the consequences of leaving that veil on have become too great.

There is a story about a kabbalist in Egypt, who was very close to the sultan, although the sultan's advisors didn't like that. They wanted to keep the sultan under their control; not have him under the influence of this spiritual guru. In front of the sultan, the advisors asked the kabbalist if it was possible to change the nature of a cat. He said, "You can't change a cat. A cat is a cat."

They brought out a cat they had trained for months to act like a servant. They clapped their hands and the cat, dressed in formal clothing, brought in a bottle of wine for a drink before dinner. Then the cat brought in the first course. Whatever they requested, the cat brought out. The advisors were happy because they believed they were creating doubt in the sultan and he would no longer want the company of his spiritual advisor. After dinner, the kabbalist went out and when he returned, he threw a mouse on the floor. The cat knocked over glasses and plates as he ran to catch the mouse. The kabbalist said, "You can dress up a cat and ask it to change its behavior, but a cat is a cat."

Our job is to transform our nature. If we come into this world and leave without correcting our garbage, we would be just like the cat—following our reactive instincts. Remember, our instinct is the Desire to Receive for the Self Alone. That's what we're being asked to change. We're being asked to transform our core nature, which is selfish.

[Conclusion & Light-Work]

In times of pressure and stress, we usually see what someone is really made of, right? That's when we see someone's real temperament. Now imagine being totally stressed out. Visualize yourself, being pressured by an outside source. You've got a deadline coming up or some other circumstance that's bothering you. There are all sorts of time constraints. Watch the dialogue in your head. Are you listening to the voice of the Light? Or are you listening to the voice of the Opponent? If your buttons are being triggered, you're listening to the Opponent. But now's your chance. What could you do differently when responding to this trigger? What could you do differently to transform your inherent nature of selfishness? What are some other options? In fact, what are five things you could do differently?

Write down the five things that you could do differently in responding to stress or when your buttons are pushed under pressure. Write down some ways you can help remember to do those things.

Refer back to the Transformation Formula, which we outlined earlier. The purpose of this Formula is to remind us not to take the bait, not to become a victim, and not to believe that the obstacle is the enemy; instead it's our response—our reactive tendency—that we need to watch out for. You can put this empowering formula to use any time you feel a loss of control in your response to a person or circumstance.

Chapter 17
Removing Blockages

In the last chapter we looked at the circumstances and people that trigger our inherent nature and found five alternate ways to negotiate these situations. You probably discovered that there are other ways to handle stress, aside from kicking and screaming or shutting down. Fortunately, we can learn to override our conditioning and handle stress proactively.

Our reactive, inherent qualities are that of a vessel—we are selfishly looking to receive. Under stress, we look for instant gratification. We worry, panic, freak out, or become victims. All of that gives us a temporary sense of release, but these responses are aspects of our garbage. But when we choose to use the Transformation Formula, stress can actually help us grow by motivating or pushing us to go to the next level. We learn not to react to challenges, obstacles, and stress as if they were the problem, but instead, we see that it's the way we respond to the stress that will determine the result: chaos or fulfillment, garbage or gifts.

Getting to the Core Seed Level

Let's say that you tend to be an impatient person; you're easily distracted and not a great listener, either because you're not interested or you don't have the patience. That's garbage. So what do you do when you feel your patience start to run thin? You restrict. You restrict your desire to be impatient, to become distracted, and to get out of that situation as soon as possible. Respecting and caring for someone means that you invest in that person's time. So, a big part of restriction for you is to just listen; people need to express themselves to feel understood and for us to understand where they are coming from.

We're talking about being proactive, sharing, and going out of our comfort zone. We're not talking about doing the "right" or moral thing. It's not about being a good, spiritual person. It's about doing the most difficult thing that we can do: breaking habits and patterns.

This is *Tikkun*.

I'll give you an example. There is a couple I used to teach, students that came to me who were both particularly selfish. They had been married about eight years. And it had become a grind. It was a relationship with no consciousness, no awareness—just two roommates with no real connection to one another. The husband was lazy, and the wife was needy and a complainer. I gave them a homework assignment. For one full week, the husband had to take care of whatever his wife asked for. If she needed something from the grocery store, he would go get it. If she needed him to clean up around the house, he would do it. If she needed him to help the kids with their homework, he would do it. But, more importantly, he would have to do it without question, comment, or challenge. He had to give unconditionally. Imagine the resistance I received as I explained this assignment!

A week later, they came back. Who do you think had the more difficult time with the assignment? The wife. Because she didn't for one second trust him to do those things correctly. He always did a good job because he was a people pleaser, but she had a hard time allowing him to take care of these tasks. In fact, she had a long-standing pattern of not counting on him, not trusting him. But at the same time, she longed to have him take care of her, to be sensitive and aware of her needs, and to make her feel good.

The following week, their roles were reversed. She had to take care of all of his needs and he had to allow her to do it. It was during that second assignment that things started to open up. She realized how dependent she had become and how she had stopped being an initiator in her life. And he realized how limited their relationship had become and how much he appreciated the things she did. By the end of the two weeks, they had both discovered how little effort each of them had been putting into their relationship after all these years. They also saw the amazing results they could produce when they took the time to do the work required.

Getting Out of Our Comfort Zone

We are so easily drawn into patterns of laziness. When we start a relationship, we're always doing thoughtful things, but we soon fall into an easy, idle routine. To change this pattern requires discipline. It requires that we switch our mindset from: *What can I do for me?* to *What can I do for you?* By focusing on what we can do for another, when our habit has been to be self-seeking, we dramatically change the dynamic of the relationship.

The first step in removing our garbage is to seek out the polar opposite of whatever issue we have. Going to extremes is rarely a prescribed course of action, but in order to achieve balance, and start removing some of our blockages, we have to go to the extreme. If your problem is laziness, try to get up at five A.M. for a week. During the work day, go against your natural tendency to surf the net. Initiate a project instead. If your nature is to ignore people, stop and listen to what every single person has to say, whether it's the clerk at the bank or the waiter at the restaurant.

How many times do we go to a restaurant, and we can't remember what our waiter looks like or what he or she is wearing. We have no idea which waiter is ours, because, for us, he or she is not even in our movie but just there to get us our food. The problem starts with not noticing our waiter and ends up with us not noticing or listening to our partner or spouse. Wherever you are, whatever your issue is, whatever you've written down in your journal, whatever your blockages are, go and seek out the opposite. Then you can say: "Wow! So this is what it feels like not to be lazy!" When you have that realization, then you can start looking for some balance.

So one way to remove blockages is to identify the problem and go to the opposite extreme for a week. Write down one thing you need to transform—your laziness, your blockage, your reactivity—and do exactly the opposite, the proactive quality. If you tend to be a procrastinator and avoid doing errands, then every day this week get up early and go get things done. Check them off your list. Who cares how you feel? This work is not based upon your emotions or your moods. It's based upon a call to action. That's what this is all about.

If you tend to be the kind of person who always waits for your partner or friends to make plans before you decide what you're going to do this weekend, then make a plan now and execute that plan. Make the reservation for dinner. Plan the weekend getaway. Plan the fishing trip. Reserve the log cabin. Get the rental car. Instead of waiting for others to provide for you, be the one to initiate.

Write down in your journal that one step you need to take regarding the one aspect of your life that you need to completely transform. Every day this week, put energy into completely transforming that aspect of your life. Get out of your comfort zone and at the end of a week, notice how you feel. This is a very powerful exercise, and I think you will find that it was well worth the effort. Hopefully, you will be able to extend these actions beyond a week. But for now, just see what it's like not to be ruled by routine or by how you happen to feel in the morning.

One of the things that you may notice as you're doing these exercises, particularly this exercise, is that your friends, family, and the people around you will notice there's something unusual happening with you. You're not acting like you normally act. Don't be surprised if their reactions and responses to you are not all positive. People can feel threatened and confused by change. But their negative reactions are actually a good sign! It means that there is real change happening, that the Opponent is starting to get busy, trying to discourage you from making a shift in consciousness, trying to keep you from changing. As you do these exercise assignments, make a note of people's reactions, write them down even, but don't lose sight of the bigger picture: your goal is to transform your nature. If no one is commenting that you're changing, it probably means you're not changing.

Working Through the Pain

Before we got on a spiritual path, we judged and hurt others. We lived selfishly, thinking only about ourselves much of the time. As a result, there are people who were left hurt in the wake of our reactive, selfish path. One of the reasons for the blockages we have in our life is to show us the pain we've caused others with our reactive responses. Therefore, one of the ways we can remove a blockage is by recognizing and experiencing that pain and discomfort for ourselves.

The Laws of the Universe say that whatever we do comes back to us. This means that we will always have an opportunity in our lives to feel the pain that we have caused others. We can also do this proactively by choosing to feel the pain we've created in people's lives now instead of receiving it from the Universe. In this way, the Universe helps to remove our blockages because of our selfless desire to remove the pain we have caused.

Let me illustrate. There's a very common experience that we all realize is uncomfortable, but we're perfectly willing to do: going to the gym. What's our purpose in going to the gym? We want to be healthier. We want to get stronger. We want to build stamina, endurance. Yet the only way that we can improve our fitness, health, and strength is by going through some discomfort. In fact, the only way we know we've done a good job is if our muscles are sore the next day.

If you knew nothing about fitness and lifted weights for the first time, the next day you'd wake up and think you'd broken something, pulled a muscle, or torn something. The reality is that you *have* torn something: microscopic muscle fibers, and the next morning they are in the process of rebuilding themselves even stronger. That's how we build muscle. It works the same for running; we build up stamina by stretching our cardiovascular limits one work-out at a time. It can't be done without some discomfort.

And yet, when we talk about emotional change and the development of emotional strength, we're unwilling to go through that kind of discomfort because we misunderstand the process. Whereas we see physical discomfort as a good sign, if something is emotionally uncomfortable, we shy away from it. But in order to get to a place of being healthier, stronger, and more resilient emotionally, we have to be willing to tolerate discomfort.

At a kabbalistic wedding ceremony, the sages will say that what counts is not how much you love someone when you're head over heels; it's how much you love them when you hate them. This always struck me as a very simple bit of wisdom. When we're in love, of course it's easy. But what about when someone is really bugging us and showing us their worst side? How much tolerance, acceptance, and love do we have when the other person is being unreasonable and demanding? Maybe your partner is sick and hasn't stopped whining for hours. Not only is this annoying, but you wanted to go on a fishing trip and now you have to stay home and take care of her. Yes, you're upset, but this is a huge growth opportunity. Kabbalistically, it's a chance to practice restriction, a chance to do the opposite of what you want to do, a chance to act unselfishly.

In the 1996 Olympics in Atlanta, I remember watching Kerri Strug, the gymnast who severely hurt her ankle during the team competition against Team Russia. The Americans were in the running for the gold, and Kerri knew she needed to go to the next level physically and psychologically to make this happen. She remembered her training, where she had performed the move hundreds of times. She had even been trained to overcome pain, but practice is one thing. It's another when you're at the Olympics and the gold medal is on the line, not just for you, but for your whole team. Despite her pain, she nailed the vault and stuck the landing with the injured ankle and elevated the consciousness of everyone watching that day.

There was a purpose to Strug's being willing to override the pain, and that purpose was greater than even winning her own medal.

In that moment, she was doing it for the greater good. She gave up her own personal ambitions of gold to bring a gold medal home for her team, and to demonstrate to the world that extraordinary possibilities arise when we think outside of our limitations.

Now, this talk of pain is not to suggest for a minute that sitting in our pain and discomfort is inherently a good thing. Enduring pain and discomfort must have a purpose, and that purpose needs to be transformative in nature. We do it in order to break the limitations of the ego and move to the next level.

And growth doesn't always have to be about overcoming pain—more often than not, it's about overcoming mere discomfort or inconvenience, like being willing to tolerate impatience while sitting bumper to bumper on the freeway stuck in traffic. It's even more uncomfortable and painful when we're missing a crucial meeting or our job is at risk. It's not like we can get airlifted out of there, so we'll have to sweat this one out. We have to learn how to breathe into the discomfort. We do this by becoming aware of the growth opportunity that is present. What can we do? There is nothing we can do in the 1 Percent realm, but by altering our thoughts, our consciousness, we can change our entire reality.

One thing to note as we start evolving, as we start progressing spiritually, is that the Opponent will prompt us to judge other people spiritually. We think we're elevated, but there are six billion people in this world—and six billion paths. People have different garbage, and different ways they will reveal their Light. No one is the same. Just because something is easy for me doesn't mean it's easy for somebody else. Conversely, something that's hard for you is not necessarily hard for someone else. We simply can't compare our path to somebody else's. Judgment is not a part of the Light; it's part of the ego.

Even restriction—going against our nature—is not the same for every person. For example, there are always some people in a Kabbalah class who will jump out of their seats in order to share or ask questions, and they are also the ones who always have an answer. They enjoy participation. For such a person, practicing restriction would be allowing other people the opportunity to ask a question or to participate. For them, it's really difficult to sit quietly.

Someone else in the class may be intimidated by being in a group of fifty or sixty people, so they stay quiet during the whole ten weeks. For that person, it would be tremendously uncomfortable to stand up in front of the whole class and share something, or give an answer that could be wrong and having others think that they don't know what they're talking about. In this case, speaking up would be practicing restriction.

Again, our level of discomfort is relative to the individual. We all have a reactive nature, but we also have the ability to know what proactive action we need to take. It's a bit like going to the dentist. It's not something that most people get excited about; we feel cautious and a bit apprehensive. But after we have gone and experienced a little discomfort, we love the way our teeth shine. The doctor didn't actually harm us—not at all—he or she helped us to have a healthier smile.

One of the things that we need to do is desensitize ourselves to being uncomfortable. We're conditioned to seek pleasure. Our vessel is hedonistic; it's pleasure-seeking by default. The idea of being uncomfortable seems unappealing, so we run away from responsibility. We run away from pressure, stress, intimacy, but these are the pathways to expanding the vessel and having more lasting fulfillment.

[Light-Work]

Remember this very simple nugget of wisdom from Kabbalah: wherever we're seeking temporary fulfillment in our life now, we may have lasting chaos. Wherever we are willing to put up with temporary discomfort now, we have a good chance of having lasting fulfillment. In other words, if you're already feeling uncomfortable in some area of your life, it's a good sign. You're on the pathway toward fulfillment.

Fear is a good barometer to gauge where we are in our level of comfort or discomfort. The more afraid that we become, the greater chance that we're getting out of our comfort zone. As part of your Light-Work, pick a fear you know you have—your biggest fear that needs to be confronted. Write down in your journal what that fear is and how it prevents you from growing and moving forward.

Make an effort to confront that fear this week. Let's say that you need to confront your boss about the raise she promised you six months ago but has failed to bring up the subject since then.

You've allowed the topic to go unaddressed, but now it's time to overcome your hesitation. Go talk to her: *By the way, remember when we talked six months ago about a raise?*

Maybe you hate heights or have a fear of flying. I have a friend who had a huge phobia about flying. He avoided flying for ten years, until he decided he was ready to confront it. He asked if I would accompany him on a short plane trip from L.A. to San Diego. I fly all the time, so it's no big deal. Yet, what a proactive step it was for him to get on a plane and go through the discomfort of sitting there as the plane took off! It was a pleasure to be able to support him in that process. So whether it's fear of rejection, confrontation, speaking in public, flying—whatever you have that keeps you stuck and potentially paralyzed—your Light-Work is to pick that fear and start to confront it. Become willing to be uncomfortable and face it.

As you write about this fear in your journal, I want you to write *when* you're going to confront it. When are you going to have that conversation with the boss? When are you going to get on that plane? When are you going back to the gym to deal with that weight problem? Be specific. When are you going to schedule that?

Remember, we're not talking about instantaneously transforming something that has kept you stuck for many years. But through this Light-Work, we're taking the edge off the pressure. We're making progress instead of remaining immobilized by our fear. All of the effort that you're putting forth to confront it means you are making tremendous strides toward overcoming it completely.

Ultimately, you will be able to turn this fear into a gift, into Light, and into fulfillment. That is our purpose.

Please don't shy away from this Light-Work. It's tough. It's uncomfortable. It will require tremendous support and encouragement from others, and it may take a few false starts before you have the courage to conquer it. But don't continue to Chapter 18 until you've taken some action to face your worst fear.

Chapter 18
Elevating Consciousness

An essential part of transforming garbage is being willing to experience discomfort. Your Light-Work was to look at aspects of your life where you have fears that paralyze you or keep you from taking action, and to start confronting them. Specifically, you were asked to schedule a time for confrontation. Did you mark your calendar?

Wherever you are in this program, continue to go back and fulfill those commitments that you made: to look at where the 1 Percent reality is limiting you, to notice signs in your life where the 99 Percent is sending you messages, to do the opposite of what's comfortable to you for one week, and to confront something that you're afraid of. These are all very important steps in our journey.

Negativity

Consciousness is more than just intellect, perception, ideas, and the sum of all cognitive functioning. Consciousness has to do with a certain frequency that we tune into. There is the consciousness of the 99 Percent realm and there is the consciousness of the 1 Percent realm. Our goal, of course, is to go beyond the limited 1 Percent realm, because this realm will never provide us with lasting fulfillment and nourishment. Where are we in our consciousness? How do you know where you are? And what are some signs that you're evolving in consciousness?

When we speak of changes in consciousness, it reminds me of a story about a man who was battling his demons. He knew he wanted to change so he sought out a great kabbalist he had heard about from a friend. He went to the kabbalist's house, a shack, and knocked on the door. The kabbalist came out and the man didn't want to look at him because all he saw was blackness surrounding the kabbalist. It wasn't the kabbalist who was emitting the darkness, however, it was his own negativity separating him from the kabbalist. He looked at the kabbalist's kids and they looked like orphans who hadn't been cared for; the wife looked like an old hag. He then managed to overcome his revulsion enough to ask the kabbalist for an action plan to work on his negativity.

He came back a few weeks later. Wow! The kabbalist's house looked clean and pretty; it practically glowed. The kabbalist came out, and he, too, was glowing. The man saw the kids, who looked like angels, and the wife was gorgeous now. He turned to the kabbalist and said: "How did you change so much in such a short time? Everything was so dark and ugly before."

The kabbalist said, "It's all in your perception of reality. Before you couldn't see beyond your own negativity, and everything was filtered through it. Now that you're on a path of change, you're beginning to get a glimpse of the true nature of the Universe."

How do you know when you have had a shift in perception? When you are able to see the beauty that surrounds you instead of darkness and chaos. One of the fundamental Laws of the Universe is the Law of Affinity, that *like attracts like*. That's true for consciousness. If we tend to be depressed, if we tend to be cynical, a bit negative, we're going to draw situations that are also negative and depressing. If we can learn to see the beauty and the good that surrounds us, we will continue to attract more good and beautiful things.

Your Universe will always be a reflection of where your consciousness is. There is no way we can trick the Universe. We can't pull one over on the Light. We have to be willing to own that our consciousness, the frequency we operate on—will always manifest a Universe that matches it.

Signs That We Are Changing

One of the clues that we're evolving is that we don't take everything so seriously, and that includes ourselves. We don't get too wrapped up in the drama of life; we allow life to be a journey. Remember, we create our own journey, our own movie. So, rather than demanding our money back when there is a scene we don't like, we can ask: *Why is this in my movie?* If there is any aspect of the movie that we're not satisfied with, then we're the ones who have to change it. One of the most important signs that our consciousness is elevating is that we're constantly looking for the lesson; constantly looking to see what we can change and improve in ourselves and in our movies.

The second thing that you may notice when your consciousness is beginning to evolve is that the things that used to bother you don't bother you as much anymore. Our buttons don't get pushed like they used to. We may still have a problem with impatience, but when we go to the bank and there is a long line, we're not freaking out, or complaining. We know it's going to take some time. We're still a little bit irritated, but now we find other ways to busy ourselves instead of complaining. This is a shift in consciousness.

The third thing is that you may notice is that it's easier to be kinder and more tolerant of others. Again, we're still going to have our buttons pushed at times. People are still going to irritate us, but we're more tolerant. It's easier to be around people. We are able to spend more time with the people who used to set us off. We're beginning to have a bit more flexibility. We're beginning to be able to compromise more. There is more flow in our relationships.

Another sign that we're evolving is that it's easier for us to communicate with people. We share more of ourselves. We allow ourselves to be vulnerable more often, and in turn we allow others to do the same with us. We become less fearful and more open with others, and, as a result of our improved communication with others, we feel more genuine and less lonely.

Yet another indication that we're evolving in our consciousness is that we become more aware of other people's feelings. We are more conscientious of how we treat others. We're aware that the words we choose can be hurtful at times. We're paying more attention to people's expressions and other non-verbal forms of communication. Kabbalists say that every living thing has a Soul and every living thing has an angel that supports it. We become more like these supporting angels.

Another sign that we are evolving is that we start to see beauty everywhere. We start to recognize and appreciate nature and all that the Creator has made available to us—the beauty of people, flowers, trees. How many times do we take a drive through the countryside and we're so wrapped up in our worries and thoughts that we're oblivious to the wildlife and beauty around us? We don't notice the coastline anymore. We don't look at the waterfalls. One of the ways that we can recognize that our consciousness is shifting is that we begin to notice *and appreciate* our surroundings. We become grateful for the people in our life. We start to realize that there are people at work who we've never spoken to, and we start to understand that they also have lives. We want to learn more about others for the simple joy in it. The 99 Percent becomes apparent in everything that we're doing and everything that we're seeing.

Probably one of the greatest indicators that we're evolving is that we are experiencing increasing resistance and opposition in our lives. The Opponent is trying hard to discourage us and to keep us from noticing the beauty that surrounds us. We might be encountering more negative situations, more people trying to put doubt in our mind, more people questioning our actions and motives. You might be hearing more comments like: *You used to be so much more fun; now you've become so spiritual and self-righteous.* These are tests, opportunities for growth, chances to practice proactive behavior. Remember the purpose of the Opponent, the ego, is to prevent us from evolving. When the Opponent is on high alert, this is a good sign indicating that change is really taking place.

Opposition to Change

We have to allow ourselves to go through these changes, knowing that we're "under construction." We haven't completed the building yet. It's still a hardhat area, not ready to welcome people to a grand reopening party. We're stripping away and we're rebuilding. And, remember that every spiritual movement meets opposition. Any form of spirituality is open to ridicule, speculation, and opposition, because the Opponent wants to stop the evolution of thought. The Opponent wants to stop people from seeking the Light.

When Christianity began, how many apostles were there with Jesus? Today there are a billion people following the Christian tradition. There was opposition to Moses in the Bible. There was opposition to the prophet Muhammad. There has been opposition to every single large shift of consciousness in the history of man. The Opponent fights tirelessly against change.

Once we're been shown something, once the veil of the Universe has been pulled back and we've seen the workings of Universal Laws, it's very difficult to go back to ignorance. Once we learn something, it's very difficult to unlearn it; once we've had an experience, it's hard to go back to being naïve. We may forget information and we may forget what it is we're here to work on, but we never forget our experiences. We never forget what we've seen.

Think of a child who is traveling on a plane for the first time. He might be given a tour of the pilot's cockpit with all its dials and the flashing lights. Whereas the child once thought of a plane as a magical thing, he begins to see that it is really just a complex machine that relies on pilots to keep it soaring through the sky. Once the child has been shown the workings of the plane, it's difficult to go back to the naïve notion that the plane flies itself. In the same way, once we're shown how the Universe works, we can't go back to a state of not knowing. We might want to put our head back in the sand, but it's never going to fit that snugly again.

We're always going to be disturbed in some way by consciousness. We're going to remember that, according to law of cause and effect, we are the cause of everything in our reality. We are the writers of our own movie script. We'd love to believe that someone else is to blame, but we've learned, according to Universal Law, that we can never believe in the "suddenly syndrome" again. There is a cause for every effect we see or experience first hand.

It's tempting sometimes to go backwards, to forget. It's tempting to try to devolve our consciousness. We're human and we're built of that Desire to Receive for the Self Alone. Of course we have the free will to go backwards. But as our desire to transform gets stronger, it becomes more difficult to allow ourselves to fall back and feel okay about it. We may well slip back, but if we have a true desire to change, we will always catch ourselves from falling.

The Logic of Illogic

According to Kabbalah, what we think is logical is totally illogical. And what we think doesn't make sense is usually what makes the most sense in life. Some of the things that we've already discussed are not really logical. Going against our nature? Seeking out embarrassing situations? Who in their right mind would put on a clown suit and walk through a town? Being willing to have people disapprove of us? This is an insane, illogical way of thinking. And, yet, that's how we elevate our lives.

There is a story about these two guys who went to a sage. One had a financial problem and the other had a severe skin rash. They asked the kabbalist about their problems and then a messenger came back with the answers, but the messenger accidentally switched the two notes. The person with the financial problem read that he should rub a special oil on his skin three times a day. The person with the skin disease was told to go into the lumber business. He thought, "This kabbalist is out of his mind!"

Meantime, the guy with the financial problem thought the kabbalist knew something he didn't know and started to put the oil on his skin three times a day. Three months later, the guy ended up striking deal after deal after deal, and became very successful. This man was open to something that was beyond him, something illogical. He allowed himself to let go of his limited way of thinking and, in return, he received exactly what he asked for.

The other guy was still stuck with his skin disorder. Unlike the guy with the financial problem, he was not willing to change his profession—become uncomfortable—and trust that whatever he did was necessary to remove his rash.

All of the possible solutions to any problem we might have already exist and are available to us. But our limiting beliefs prevent us from knowing them. The fact that we limit our ability to understand does not limit the wisdom itself. That which is illogical only seems that way because we haven't wrapped our minds around it yet.

The *Zohar*, the text of Kabbalah written centuries ago, talks about the seven continents, despite the fact that the existence of the continents was not known when the text was written. It talks about the world being round, for which there was no evidence up until five hundred years ago. Abraham talked about the wisdom of astrology four thousand years ago. How can this be? It's not logical. But logic has never brought about lasting answers, or lasting fulfillment. How many engineers or mathematicians have chaos in their lives because logic is not the solution? The solution lies in understanding that there is wisdom that exists which is much greater than our ability to comprehend it with our 1 Percent minds. But, if we let go, if we tap into the unlimited potential of fulfillment, we can access this wisdom.

When enough people in this world become elevated, we will reach a critical mass. When that happens, a huge shift will take place in the world. Everyone's perception will be different. There will be breakthroughs in science and technology, as well as in medicine—breakthroughs that are only distant dreams today. Our goal is not only to change ourselves, it's to become part of universal transformation. As we elevate, the Universe elevates. We need to believe that we're part of a movement of change. We have a global responsibility. When we change, we help change the world.

[Light-Work]

In order to understand this notion of critical mass, Rav Ashlag, the founder of the Kabbalah Centre in 1922 in Jerusalem, gave a very simple analogy. Place on one side of a balance scale sesame seeds that represent chaos, darkness, pain and suffering in the world, and on the other side place sesame seeds that represent unlimited fulfillment, joy, happiness, and the removal of all pain and suffering. Rav Ashlag then asked the question: How many seeds would it take to tip the scale one way or the other? The answer is one. And that's what critical mass means to us. That seed could be one action of caring—one person deciding to make a difference, one vote that tips the scale in an election.

Too often we believe that who we are is not enough, that our gestures of kindness and love won't make a difference, and that our ability to restrict and control our ego won't mean a thing in the grand scale of things. Yet, according to the kabbalists, just one action can mean the difference between darkness and Light.

As your Light-Work, think about what that one sesame seed would be for you. What is that one action, gesture, or change that you need to make that could potentially tip the scales from darkness and chaos to Light and fulfillment? This is a very deep question: *What could tip the scales in your personal critical mass from garbage to gift, from darkness to light, from selfishness to unconditional giving?* Really give this some thought and write down your answer in your journal. Don't be satisfied with an easy answer. Allow yourself to go to a deeper level. Be sure to give yourself enough time to decide what that one change would be that could be the tipping point for you and your life.

Chapter 19
The Light

We've been chipping away, trying to get to the cause of all of our pain, limitations, negativity, and self-defeating patterns. We have been working hard to root out our blockages and get to a place where we can be unlimited, where we can experience true freedom and happiness. We've been using the following terms interchangeably: the Light, the Creator, God, our higher power, energy, the 99 Percent. There is nothing more important in this Universe than the concept of the Light, so let's slow down for a minute and really understand what this term means.

Remember our analogy from Rav Ashlag about the sesame seeds on the scale? On one side, there were seeds that represented darkness, chaos and negativity, and on the other side, we had seeds that represented Light, joy, happiness and fulfillment. We agreed that it only takes one seed on either side of the scales to tip those scales. This analogy brings us to our purpose for being in the world: to tip the scales toward fulfillment, joy, and happiness. Did you do your Light-Work to identify your tipping point? What was that one action that you need to make in order to tip those scales? Finding fulfillment lies in the answer you wrote down.

The Light Being Part of the 99 Percent

Let's assume for a moment that we've done our Light-Work and tipped the scales toward the Light. We've come out of the darkness successfully, and arrived at a sense of illumination. What does it mean to be enlightened, to have Light? What does that really feel like, and how do we know when we've arrived?

In the very first session of any introductory Kabbalah course, we always begin by explaining the whole notion of fulfillment and Light, of the 99 Percent realm. Yet, here we are, nineteen chapters into the book, and we're explaining it in detail for the first time. Why? Because the Light is a complex concept. We can begin to grasp the ideas of light and darkness, but to truly know what it means to experience Light on an energetic level can take lifetimes. Kabbalists have explained to us that we can never truly conceptualize God; it's beyond our ability even to intellectualize the whole notion. Instead, they give us the metaphor of Light to help bridge the gap.

Imagine that you're standing at the ground level of the Empire State Building, but the whole structure is made of wax. It's a giant candle, hundreds of stories high. From where you are on street level, can you see the lit wick of that candle, hundreds of stories up? No, it's impossible. What we see is the light emanating from this vast candle, the light that comes from the burning wick. When we talk about the Light, we're really talking about the Light that emanates from God. And from where we are in this Universe, we cannot touch God; we cannot see God; we cannot conceptualize God. But we can understand or have a sense of the Light that comes from God.

Kabbalists understand this and so they give us the notion of the Light, or that which emanates from the Creator and fills us up. The Light is felt when we are inspired or excited, when we feel love, joy, and happiness, and when we create. These are experiences that we can all relate to. On the flip side, we see darkness. Most of us are intimately familiar with this notion, as well. Darkness is the absence of Light.

On a physical level, physicists once thought of light as waves. Then they thought of light as a stream of particles. Now they see light as being sometimes a wave and sometimes a stream of particles. The physical manifestation of light changes because light is energy, and energy takes on different forms.

Scientists are realizing that we can't understand this physical world until we go back to the seed. Quantum physics, metaphysics, and the like attempt to understand matter at its most fundamental level, so that we can one day prove physically what kabbalists have known all along: that everything in this physical world emanates from a non-physical reality.

Brief Personal History

In 1922, Rav Ashlag established the Kabbalah Centre in order to have a forum for people who wanted to connect to the Light and gain fulfillment. He passed away in 1955 and his student, Rav Brandwein, my father's teacher, took over the leadership of the Kabbalah Centre. In 1969, my father's master passed away, and my father then became the leader of the Kabbalah Centre. Weeks later, he met my mom and told her about his involvement with Kabbalah. My mom was always a spiritual seeker, into meditation and Eastern forms of spirituality. She was intrigued by my father's knowledge of Kabbalah, and she immediately asked to be taught. She even offered to work for the Centre for free.

My father was unsure, so they decided to meet again at a certain restaurant in Manhattan to make his decision or in this case, get his answer. When they met again, my father was depressed and down. Before he said anything, my mother said: "I have to tell you a dream I had last night. In my dream, I was visited by an older man with a cane, coat, and hat." She described my father's departed teacher, Rav Brandwein, exactly. "Then he tapped me on the head and disappeared."

My dad, instead of being depressed, was now shining. He said, "Last night, before I went to sleep, I asked my teacher to come to me in a dream, to tell me if I could teach you Kabbalah. I was coming today to say I couldn't teach you because he didn't come to me. But instead of coming to me, he came to you."

And that's how they started their relationship. If it hadn't been for my mom, a small group of scholars would probably be living in Jerusalem learning Kabbalah through the night, but none of us would have ever been exposed to the wisdom of Kabbalah. My mom came from a secular background and thus believed that no one should be allowed to limit this information. She believed that anything that's true should be shared, and that anyone should be able to study Kabbalah. Since that moment, the gates of Kabbalah have been opened to everyone. That's why there are millions of people around the world studying Kabbalah right now.

Once You Know, You Can't Turn Back

There is a very profound story about a student standing at a window with his master, who is pointing out the window. They're standing there for hours. Then the master leaves and the student remains at the window, sobbing. His peers ask him: "What's going on? Why are you so emotional? What's happening?"

The student says, "My master was showing me all the Light that the world is ready for—all of the potential fulfillment, joy, and happiness within each of us. And the unlimited fulfillment that is available."

They said, "That's amazing. But why are you so sad? Why such heaviness?"

He said, "Well, although he showed me all the Light and the potential fulfillment that's available, I also see all the darkness that we must overcome before that Light can be revealed—all the pain and suffering, missed opportunities, and limitations."

This student has realized a powerful truth: yes, there is endless Light in this Universe, but we have to go through the process of earning that Light, and that is difficult.

What if we don't make it? What if we're not willing to go through the discomfort of breaking out of our limitations? What if we allow our egos to control us? The answer is that you have already made it. Just by opening up this book and opening yourself up to the beautiful wisdom of Kabbalah, you have revealed a bit of Light. Your life is already more illuminated than it was before you began this journey. And once you've experienced that Light, it's very difficult to pretend that it doesn't exist. You can't go back in time. After identifying how your reactive nature harms yourself and others, you will feel a sense of urgency about removing that darkness from your life.

When we turn on a light in a darkened room, every corner of that room is illuminated. In other words, the light doesn't shine on only half or three-quarters of the room. In fact, if you took the walls down from that room, the light would keep going. Light knows no boundaries. So we know that there is nowhere in this Universe that the Light doesn't shine; it's endless. However, at the moment we're in a game of Hide and Seek, and the Light is concealed. It is our job to uncover it. It's like a lamp in a room that you have covered with blankets—there only appears to be no light in the room.

When it's night, it's not as if the sun has gone. Its light is concealed from us because it's on the other side of the world. The sun never goes out. If it's grey and cloudy during the day, but we fly above the clouds, what do we see? Sunshine. It's always there. Just like our limitations and blockages prevent us from always experiencing the Light.

One of the best tools to help illuminate the Light inside us and make the darkness disappear is to seek out the Light in others, especially in people who annoy us or those with whom we may not have the best relationships. If we look at them and see the good—the Light inside of them—we connect with and reveal the Light inside of us. The harder it is to find the Light, the more potential there is for Light to be revealed. So seek out your mother-in-law, your co -worker, your boss—whoever that button-pushing person is—and try to find the Light inside them. The more Light we see in others, the more we'll see in ourselves.

[Light-Work]

This is probably the easiest Light-Work so far. In fact, it's really *Light-Work*. We are going to practice gratitude. Simply go to your journal and make a list of any activities through which you experience Light. In other words, write down the blessings in your life, those things for which you have great appreciation.

What are some examples of Light? The experience of singing, laughing, or dancing with joy; of being in love; of connecting or sharing with others; of inspiration, a sense of productivity, expansiveness; the emotion we feel when we play or hear beautiful music, when we look at artwork—all of these exemplify Light.

Practicing gratitude is a k-Tool designed to keep us from taking the blessings in our life for granted. How easy it can be to fall into a passive state, where all we see is the 1 Percent. We ignore the Light that we have already revealed! Remember, our purpose in life is to reveal the Light that is already there and has been there all along—not just for ourselves, but for everyone around us. As Plato said:

We can easily forgive a child who is afraid of the dark. The real tragedy is when men are afraid of the Light.

Vessel

Chapter 20
The Vessel

We are beginning to understand, on a much deeper level, the whole notion of what the Light is and how it manifests in this physical world. In your last Light-Work assignment, you had the opportunity to list activities in which you experience the Light–through singing, painting, music, and your kids, for example. You were able to see the Light that already exists in your life.

Whether you knew it or not, any time you have ever experienced the Light, you were acting as a container. To capture the fulfillment that flows from the Universe, there must always be a container. Otherwise it's a bit like a pitcher pouring water. With no cup or glass to receive it, the water creates a puddle, a mess of chaos on the floor.

In other words, we need a vessel to receive the Light. Our nature, when we come into this world, is to be a container of Light. So what makes a vessel?

Remember that being a vessel starts with desire. Spiritual Light does not show up in this Universe unless there is a desire to contain it.

Sharing & Greed

To illustrate the need for our desire or the expansion of our desire, we turn to a story about a Ukrainian kabbalist, called the Baal Shem Tov, who lived several centuries ago. He came to a family and asked if he could stay for dinner. They were very excited by the prospect of this great kabbalist coming to their house for dinner, but the Baal Shem Tov had some demands. He wanted to have a five-course meal—with beef, and wanted all of his students to be fed, as well. This family had only a shack and a cow—the sum total of all of their possessions—but they kept their concerns to themselves.

The poor man went to the market and slaughtered his cow, which he prepared for the Baal Shem Tov's five-course meal. He sold his shack so he could have enough food for the students. The Baal Shem Tov arrived and when the food was placed before him, he devoured everything, making sure there was nothing left.

In the morning, the Baal Shem Tov left and the head of the family remembered that he no longer had a cow and his shack was about to be transferred to the person who bought it. So he went into the forest and said: "God, My family has nothing. Please provide us with some source of sustenance. We were drinking the cow's milk and making it into cheese and that was our only food. Now we have no cow's milk and no cheese. Please, please, I beg you. Give me fulfillment." Through his tears, he saw a bundle lying on the ground near him. When he opened the bundle, he found it was full of gold coins. He suddenly realized that if the Baal Shem Tov hadn't taken their cow and house, he would never have gone into the forest, begged for help, and found the coins. In that moment, he became a very wealthy man.

The point of the story is that we become accustomed to our limited vessel, but great fulfillment awaits us if only we had a larger vessel in which to stow it. We need to dig down deep and figure out if we are unintentionally keeping our vessel small. *Am I limiting what I can accomplish? Am I thinking small? Can my vessel be expanded?* In essence, that is what the Baal Shem Tov revealed to the man in the story. His actions showed the poor man that the Universe had so much more to offer him if he would just open his eyes and his vessel.

Like the man who fell to his knees crying and begging for God to help, sometimes we have to hit bottom before we see clearly. But this isn't always the case. It's not necessary for us to hit a crisis point before we grow, but if a crisis is what is needed to wake us up from our slumber, that is what the Universe will provide.

Students will often tell me: "But I didn't hit bottom yet." That's an ego statement. We have some idea that we're supposed to crash and burn before we appreciate what we have. Why do we think that we need to be in absolute darkness in order to appreciate the Light? That's like saying we need to suffer profoundly in order to be free of pain. It's simply not true, and it's a very limited way of thinking. One doesn't have to be penniless in order to have the desire for abundance. The real question is this: *How can I decide today, within my own consciousness, that I've had enough, that this is my turning point?* If you want to keep digging to China, knock yourself out. But you can also decide today that you're done with the self-ishness. You're through with your limited way of thinking. You've had enough unsatisfying relationships. You're tired of smoking. Or you don't want to be broke anymore. Cultivate a sense of urgency right now—in this moment.

The older we get, the more urgency there is to want to leave a lega-cy, to do something that's going to make an impression in this world. When we're twenty, who cares? It's all about excitement and experiencing life fully and having fun. But the older we get, the more responsibility we feel—the more need we have to accomplish our life's work. But, your age shouldn't matter. It's never too early or too late to satisfy your life's purpose: finding fulfillment and reveal-ing the Light of that fulfillment to everyone.

Some might contend that finding fulfillment is a selfish endeavor. It's only selfish when we Desire for the Self Alone. How can we tell if this is our intention? We ask: *Why do I want to draw to myself real lasting joy and happiness?* If we have a desire to receive fulfillment should we covet it, and not share it with others, of course, that's selfish. But when our intention, our desire, is to share the Light we reveal, we are in perfect alignment with the Creator. We have creat-ed affinity by acting exactly as the Creator acts. By sharing the Light we receive, we guarantee that it lasts.

If we get really good news, what do we want to do? We want to share. We want to be a channel for this positive flow of energy. How do we do that exactly? Imagine an eight-ounce cup. How much can an eight-ounce cup hold? About eight ounces of fluid, right? But if we open up the bottom of that cup and create something like a pipe, an unlimited amount of fluid can pass through our container. We all have the capacity to let an unlimited amount of Light flow through our vessel. Light is unlimited, with no beginning and no end. My understanding of being a perfect vessel is this: to have an unlimited desire for lasting joy and happiness through endless sharing.

Greed is good. In some ways, this credo has its merits. We need to want it all. We need to want to be the best we can be. There is nothing wrong with wanting everything. In this way, it's good to be "greedy." It's good to have a big desire. The problem is this: the Law of the Universe says that if you're thinking only of yourself, it's impossible to be the best person you can be. If you're thinking about yourself, you can't be truly successful. The only way to be successful is to have the well-being of others in mind. We share with others because we desire happiness for ourselves, and we know the only way to claim fulfillment for ourselves is to have others in mind.

The Rav always said that it's not about being good people. We're only good because we give of ourselves to others. If we don't have others in mind, what we do have is eventually taken away. The only way to keep what we have and to have more is to fulfill other people's needs and desires. When everyone behaves in this way, no desire is left unfulfilled. This is not a philosophy that we're talking about here. Nor is it an opinion or a judgment. It is the inherent nature of the vessel.

Two kinds of receiving

The vessel is a code word in Kabbalah for the Desire to Receive; that's our inherent nature. There is the Desire to Receive for one's Self Alone; this is also known as selfishness. Then there's the desire to receive in order to share with others, which is our goal kabbalistically. We want to be able to receive everything we possibly can, so that we can then share it and become connected to others around us. We can only share what we have. If I'm depressed, if I'm thinking small, if I'm skeptical, if I'm angry, then all I have is my anger, skepticism, and pain to pass on to others. On the other hand, if I'm excited, abundant, charismatic and energized—that energy is going to rub off on people. But we must maintain a strong vessel to be able to allow all of this positive energy to pass through us and on to others.

As long as we are acting like the Light and not acting only as the vessel, we have two capacities. We come here conditioned and built to receive, but we also have the capacity to share. What we need to do is maintain our Desire to Receive, while also adding in the ability to share. That's the secret of Kabbalah.

There are two modes to the vessel: the reactive and the proactive. The reactive mode of the vessel is its existence; you wake up in the morning and do the same habitual stuff you did yesterday. In the proactive approach of the vessel, you're thinking about what you're doing; you're aware. The way to get your vessel to be more proactive in nature is by having others in mind. If we're living this life selfishly, we're merely existing, not living.

In one of the workshops I conducted with the teachers of the Centre, I asked: "If today was the last day of your life, what legacy would you be leaving behind?" Sure, we are always running around doing this and that to get through our days, but do we really have a feeling of urgency, a sense that we need to be accomplishing big things now? I looked at the teachers and there were blank expressions on their faces, because we don't think about finishing things, owning things, building our vessel, and creating a sense of accomplishment. Our plans are always a bit vague; urgency can't gain a foothold in all this ambiguity. But what if we thought today might be the end, our last day on Earth? Then our desire to be great would be clear, because the vessel by its nature longs to expand, to grow, to move from one level to the next, to realize its potential by accomplishing great things.

[Light-Work]

It's amazing what happens when you ask yourself honestly: What have I done in this world? What did I come here to do? Am I on track? That's why I am making this exercise your Light-Work. I want you to think about your legacy. If this was your last day on Earth, what would you have left behind? What would you have accomplished? What would be meaningful? What were the missed opportunities, and what opportunities did you take? Have you gone outside of your nature to be proactive and take life on? Please take the time to write down these thoughts in your journal. This can be a great opportunity for you to be honest about where you are in your life and what you've accomplished.

Based upon what that list shows you, the second question is: What legacy would you want to leave behind? If you had an opportunity to do it over, what would you be doing instead? Now that you're living Kabbalah and understand the need to turn your garbage into gifts, what would those gifts be that you would like to offer the world? Give yourself plenty of time to answer these questions. There's no doubt; this is big stuff. You are re-creating your present and your future.

Sharing

Chapter 21
Stop Taking From Others

So, did you discover the legacy that you hope to leave for others? How does it feel to know the path that you are going to take? Your path and your legacy will become even clearer as you move further along your spiritual journey. We know that we've come here with a very specific purpose: not only to receive fulfillment, but also to share it, to connect to everyone in this world as the Light.

Part of the previous chapter was about understanding the nature of the vessel, which is inherently based upon a Desire to Receive. We have free will; we have a choice as to whether we are a passive vessel, which only receives, or whether we become a proactive vessel by adding in the quality or attribute of sharing.

What happens when we don't change our nature? We get stuck in a mode of constantly receiving. Back in Chapter 17, you were given a specific exercise to do the opposite of your nature for a week. If you were stuck in a pattern of being lazy or procrastinating, the work was to get up early in the morning and tackle your errands, for example. Now we're going to talk about what happens when we don't make any changes, when we stay stuck as a vessel that solely exists to receive.

The Grass Isn't Always Greener

We damage not only ourselves, but also all of those around us when we don't stop taking from others. When we take from others something that doesn't belong to us, we're stealing. In other words, we're stealing other people's Light. In Kabbalah, we call this the "evil eye." We look at someone and want what they have, without doing any of the work to get it. We disregard the effort needed to get that Ferrari or that healthy body. We only want the final result.

Energetically, when we want something, we take some of its Light. When we take Light in this manner, the other person gets emptied of part of his or her Light. It's one of those cosmic rules that if we have jealousy, we're taking part of somebody else's Light. We want to take one piece of somebody else's life process and throw it into our puzzle, not knowing if it fits in our big picture or not. You know what? If we're using someone else's puzzle piece for our puzzle, it's not going to fit. Not to mention that we've destroyed the other person's puzzle. Nobody benefits.

If we really were fulfilled, if we had a meaningful life with purpose and direction and focus, and if we had abundance and happiness, there would be nothing that we'd want to take from others. We wouldn't want other people's bodies, houses, cars, partners, or money. We wouldn't need these things to be happy. It's the idea that we have a lack in our lives, that something is missing, which causes us to envy what other people have. It doesn't make us evil. It doesn't make us terrible people. But whether we are aware of it or not, in some way we're taking energy from that person.

For example, imagine you're invited to the wedding of your best girlfriend, who's marrying a wonderful guy. Of course, you're happy for her, because he's like this dream guy. She has met her soul mate and it's clear that they truly love each other. You're at the wedding, but you can't help but feel envy. *What about me? How come I never meet anyone? I also have these wonderful things to offer.* It's dangerous because we can find ourselves in some way wanting to take away from our friend's experience, whether we recognize it or not. Fortunately, there is a very simple way that we can transform that judgment: *be happy for the other person.*

I have a friend who was one of those people who could never seem to meet anyone. He had five or six guys who were good friends and every one of them had a girlfriend. They were great girls. Part of him was happy for them, but another part was miserable. Whatever happened to boys' night out? His friends weren't available anymore. Rather than be upset, he felt excited because he was the last one, so he recognized that it was merely a question of time before he would meet someone.

My mom always tells a story about the Plotkin Diamond. Whoever was going out with Mr. Plotkin got to wear this huge fifty-karat diamond. The catch with the Plotkin Diamond was it came with Mr. Plotkin—who was this annoying, obnoxious person. Some women might say: "Wow! I wish I had that diamond." But when you looked at the whole picture, you saw that the person wearing the Plotkin Diamond had to live with this insufferable man. Knowing this, no one would want to put themselves in that situation no matter how big the diamond.

Sometimes we envy what others have but also see them as less than we are. It seems paradoxical, but it happens. We envy and criticize because of our own self-judgment. We tend to be our own worst enemies. Because we don't allow ourselves to experience the goodness in our own lives, we never feel adequate. We bring others down to our level in the process because it temporarily makes us feel better. It's that Capricorn quality of chasing our tails and never feeling that what we're doing is enough. As a result, we are never open to the energy of abundance. We could be working hard, but we feel little fulfillment from our work.

To help us understand where our judgment comes from, there is a story about a kingdom where everyone had a problem. No one was satisfied, so the king came up with a brilliant idea. He told all his loyal followers to go to the center of town and bring with them a list of all their possessions and everything that was good about their life. On the other side of the paper, they were to write down a list of everything they were lacking and everything that was bad. The king promised that they could exchange cards with anybody else, but they couldn't take only what the person listed on the good side; they also had to take what was on the other side. They had to take the good with the bad.

Everyone ran to the wealthiest person first. They saw how much money he had—billions and billions—but when they looked on the

other side of his piece of paper, they saw that his son was strug-
gling with addiction, and despite having a beautiful wife, the
wealthy man had chaotic relationships with various mistresses.
They all agreed that having wealth wasn't worth all of that
heartache, so they went to the most intelligent person in town. But
they saw that, despite her intelligence, she was a miserable woman
who did nothing but study night and day. Next, they ran to the most
attractive person in the community, but they saw that although he
was blessed with good looks, he never felt that he was good
enough and sometimes was too down on himself to even get out
of bed. At the end of the day, everyone went home with their own
card, content with what they had.

It's so easy to focus on what we lack. We don't realize that just
because someone has something we want, it doesn't mean he or
she is totally fulfilled. Something is probably lacking in this person's
life, too. And if there isn't something lacking, that person had to
work very hard to change their behavior, to change their consciousness, and to go to a higher level to achieve the fulfillment they now
enjoy.

We tend to project our illusions and fantasies onto other people.
This is why many people are obsessed with celebrities. But we
know that whatever glamorous idea someone has about a celebrity, it rarely coincides with the reality of that celebrity's life. In fact,
we see all the time how much chaos can come from a celebrity
lifestyle. As we know by now, true fulfillment only comes from sharing our divine gifts with the world—and this same Universal Law
holds true for everyone.

What can we do to stop inadvertently stealing energy from others, to stem our judgment and the evil eye? What are the tools we can use to transform our tendency toward jealousy and envy? As with everything we've learned in Kabbalah, the first step is to recognize that the reason we're unhappy is because we're blocked and our thinking is limited. The reason we compare ourselves to others is because we're not where *we* want to be, so we imagine that we'd be happier if we were in someone else's shoes. How many of us have wanted to be like the billionaires we read about in *Forbes* magazine, because we think that money can buy us happiness? Do you know how many millionaires and billionaires are miserable and depressed? A 1 Percent solution isn't going to change a 99 Percent issue.

Judgment and envy indicate that we're disconnected from the love of the Creator and feeling separated from others. But we know that the separation we feel is just an illusion. So what's the solution? Remember, the golden rule of Kabbalah, which is also the Golden Rule we were taught in childhood: *Love thy neighbor as thyself.* Do unto others as we would have others do to us. In other words, treat others with human dignity, respect, and care, because that is what we would want to experience for ourselves. We can't have a double standard. There is no loophole in the Universal Law that allows me to treat people selfishly, while the whole world gives me a break.

Showing others love, respect, and acceptance despite our desire to feel otherwise is one way to overcome the evil eye. Another way to rid ourselves of judgment and envy is by recognizing that we have judgment and envy in the areas where we feel we have a lack. In what aspect of your life are you missing that connection to the

99 Percent? Where do you feel empty? Where do you feel inadequate? It is in this very area you will try to draw energy from someone else. Do you find yourself thinking: *If I just had that spouse, that house, that bank account, lifestyle, suit, career, then I'd be happy...?* If so, then it's time to address why you are keeping yourself from being fulfilled in this area. It's time to put more energy into becoming fulfilled in your own career, financial situation, house, or relationship. Only then will you stop feeling resentful of others who have what you think you want.

The bottom line is this: We can't get what we want by having a fantasy about it; we have to be willing to do something about it. Success depends on our own desire for change. We have two choices in life: to do the hard work involved in the evolution of consciousness, or abdicate responsibility through judgment. It's a five-second judgment or a lifetime of work. Judgment is the easy way out, with no lasting reward.

[Light-Work and The Red String]

Consider where you are judging others, where you are focused on taking energy, and where you feel a lack. As part of your Light-Work, focus on any aspect of your life where you are envious of others, or where you're judging them, or vicariously living through them.

The second part of the Light-Work, which requires a little bit more action, is to take the person that you have the most judgment toward and do three acts of sharing for this person without telling them why you're doing it. Make them coffee. Leave flowers on their desk. Perform a kind gesture. Go completely against your nature. Again, this is a very illogical thing to do, but you will find it completely changes the flow of energy of judgment into a form of giving and sharing. When you stop taking energy from others, you can earn it for yourself.

Another way we can stop taking from others is by using a tool called the Red String, which we discussed earlier. The string is taken to Rachel's Tomb, where it's imbued with the energy to protect us from the evil eye, from other people's judgment. In the Bible, Rachel was our mother and protector, not only from physical harm, but also from spiritual harm. Our biggest spiritual threat comes from other people's envy and judgment. As kabbalists, we wear the Red String not only to protect us from other people's judgment, but also to protect us from our own. The moment a jealous or judgmental thought comes along, we can look at our wrist and remember the importance of sharing our Light, instead of taking it from others with our judgmental thoughts. We are reminded that taking from others gains us nothing. It only adds to our feelings of emptiness.

In order to help remove judgment, ask someone to tie the Red String on your wrist. We wear the Red String on our left wrist, because the left hand signifies the taker, or the receiver, while the right hand signifies the giver. Ask someone who does not have judgment toward you, someone who loves you, and has a connection with you. While tying the seven knots in the string, have the person do the brief meditation in the Red String package included.

Chapter 22
Sharing with Others

In the last chapter our Light-Work focused on what happens when we take too much energy from other people by practicing judgment and envy, or what kabbalists call the "evil eye." Were you able to identify areas in your life where you felt a lack and therefore practiced judgment of others? More importantly, did you perform three acts of sharing towards someone you envied or judged? I know it was a little bit uncomfortable or awkward, but I also know that your acts of sharing revealed much Light.

Sharing With Others

Kabbalah teaches us that relationships are not just a way to connect with people, they are actually our purpose—we must have relationships in order to make the corrections that we came into this life to make. Why? It's only through relationships with our friends, our loved ones, and our partners that our own reactive traits are revealed. Remember, the people in our life mirror back to us that which we need to correct in our own lives. And through this correction process, we learn how to reveal Light.

We understand that there are two types of receiving: the selfish Desire to Receive for the Self Alone, which, unfortunately, can end up causing us even more chaos, and the receiving that enables us to share with others. It would be great if we truly were unconditional in our sharing. It would be wonderful if we were all able to love wholeheartedly, without conditions, without holding back.

The truth is that there are reasons we come up with conditions—those terms under which we share. Why do we have conditions? It's very simple. Because we don't want to share. True sharing requires effort. It requires getting out of our comfort zone. True sharing is not contingent on our moods, hormones, or emotions, and it's not always convenient. This is because true, unconditional sharing exists in the world of the 99 percent, while our emotions and moods are a part of our physical 1 percent world. In this way, we are limited. Our feelings never stay the same. We are moody one day and happy the next. We even talk about falling in love and falling out of love. Feelings change. So the whole notion of relationships and sharing is that it's not an experience rooted in the physical/emotional plane. It's rooted in the Light, so it has to do with energy. It has to do with consciousness.

People can be very giving. They can give money, volunteer time, or even donate an entire wing of a hospital! But it's also possible that those same people end up no more fulfilled than the rest of us. They can feel bitter, resentful, hurt, insecure, depressed, and empty. How is that possible? It's such an important question. How is it possible to be a truly giving, charitable person and yet not experience fulfillment?

The Consciousness of Giving

We learn that there are different kinds of motivations and intentions in giving. Remember, we can't see consciousness. It's not always apparent. We might be able to see the wing of the hospital and the inscribed plaque on the wall. We might even see the hundreds of people who are accommodated by that hospital wing. To say that the donor was selfish wouldn't be fair. But how could it be that a person who gave so much is still in chaos after writing a check that big?

Kabbalists give us a very deep explanation.

The truth is that we don't always give with the right consciousness. Isn't it possible to give a donation for selfish reasons? Isn't it possible to want a plaque so everyone would know what we did? Sometimes we give for validation. Sometimes we give so that people will approve of us. Sometimes we give because we're insecure or because of peer pressure. We give to get special treatment or privileges. Whatever it is, there are ways that we give and reasons why we give that aren't always connected to pure sharing.

How many times do we sit in church, in a community center, or in a meeting when the hat is passed around and people start putting change and dollar bills into the collection? We usually don't hesitate to put our money in. But is it because we really feel charitable or because we don't want to be judged? Do we just feel obligated? Think about it.

We can give monetarily, physically, and emotionally, while our consciousness is still based upon the Desire to Receive for the Self Alone. That explains why, kabbalistically, we can perform acts of giving yet not change the energy in our consciousness. We give and give but we never feel fulfilled.

There is a famous story about Joseph, the Holy Miser. Everyone in town despised him, because he never shared or gave a cent to anyone. When he was about to die, the burial society said: "It's time to give, because if you're not going to give, we're not going to bury you in the cemetery. We're going to leave you on the side of the road and pile a bunch of rocks on you." He said, "I don't care. Do whatever you want."

A few days after his death, a spiritual leader of the town started getting dozens of requests for money from the town's poor people. He didn't understand why they were all suddenly coming up with requests at the same time. They said to him: "I've been receiving money for ten, twenty, thirty years. But now no more money is coming in." It suddenly hit him that these requests coincided with the death of Joseph the miser. He started asking people: "Did you have any interaction with Joseph?

It turned out that every one of the people in town at some point in their lives needed money, which eventually led them to the Holy Miser. And he was very nice to them. He sat them down and listened to their problems. They would tell him about their lives and how they needed money. But just when they thought they were about to receive his help, Joseph would start to scream at them. "You think I'm going to give you anything?" And he would throw them out. A few days later, an envelope would appear under their door with the exact amount of money they were asking for. Yet no one ever made the connection because Joseph had been so angry when he kicked them out. These stories collectively painted an amazing picture: Joseph had been sharing with the whole town but never wanted any recognition, even on his deathbed. After his death, people started calling him Joseph, the Holy Miser.

The story of Joseph has a short epilogue that I would also like to share. When Joseph arrived in heaven, he was asked: "What's it like to be up in heaven with some of the greatest Souls that ever lived?" He said, "You know what? It's an amazing blessing. But nothing compares with the sense of joy and fulfillment I used to feel every time I slipped an envelope under someone's door."

Joseph always ensured that his reason for giving was not about having his ego stroked. In fact, he went out of his way to come across as a mean, selfish person, so that his ego would be crushed. He did not want to get the recognition that would build his ego. All he wanted was to experience the pleasure of being able to help others anonymously. It's really difficult to give in this world without wanting something in return—satisfaction at the very least. And it's very hard to find opportunities when we can give with no strings attached. But Joseph found a way.

This is not to say that true giving must be anonymous. It doesn't have anything to do with anonymity, but rather with the reasons and the consciousness behind our sharing. Pure sharing is not attached to the accolades we'll receive or how popular we'll become. It doesn't have a hidden agenda. As long as we are sharing solely in order to create joy and blessings for others, we are in perfect alignment with the Light of the Creator.

Whose Money Is It?

The truth is, it's not really our money. Anything that we have is ours only to manage, which makes us money managers. Even if we have billions of dollars in our accounts, it's not really ours; we're only managing the Creator's money. That's our function. Money is energy. It's not a currency that we're trading in. We're trading in energy. And the question is: *How are we managing that energy?* After all, every time we use money we're giving away something that belongs to the Universe, so we'd better use it wisely.

There is a story about one kabbalist who, every time someone came to him with a financial problem, always sent the person to one of his wealthy students for assistance. The wealthy student would always give the individual enough money to get by. But one day the wealthy student became worried about how much money he was giving away, so he decided to stop giving away money for a while. This seemed like a prudent decision. There was a young boy sent by the kabbalist who was in desperate need of financial help, but instead of helping, the wealthy student said: "You know what? I can't help you right now." Little by little the student who used to have lots of money became poor and the boy who he had been turned away became wealthier and wealthier. Finally, the now poor student came to the master and asked: "What happened? Why did I lose everything?"

The master said, "The money was never yours. The Creator gave you the money because your mission was to be the manager of the money in order to help others. Once you decided not to share, the Creator took that blessing away from you and gave it to somebody else."

Like the once-wealthy student, all we are asked to do is manage the Creator's energy—in this case—it is in the form of money. If we feel a sense of ownership, we won't ever be able to receive the fulfillment that the Creator has for us. Because no matter how much we have in our account balance, it'll never be enough. Once we switch consciousness and realize we're only money managers, we open ourselves up to experiencing more fulfillment in all areas of our life.

True Giving

We can't stress enough that it's not the physical act of giving that is so essential; it's the consciousness behind it, the shift in our understanding of giving. There are plenty of people who give reactively, plenty of people who give thoughtlessly. We think spirituality is about being a good, kind person, but we act kindly toward others while covering up our true consciousness. And that's the reason why it's possible to still feel unfulfilled.

Our whole purpose in life is to give as the Creator does—endlessly.

How many times do you hear yourself saying: "I give too much. I'm exhausted." The truth is, it's not possible to be depleted by giving. If you feel depleted after giving, than what you did was not really giving. You had an unconscious, hidden agenda to Receive for the Self Alone, and that's why you feel such emptiness and fatigue. When you give selflessly, you will feel nothing but fullness.

There's a cute story about a letter addressed to God, written in a childish scrawl, that came to a post office. A postal employee, not knowing exactly what to do with the letter, opened it and read: "Dear God, my name is Jimmy. I'm six years old. My father is dead and my mom is having a hard time raising me and my sister. Would you please send us five hundred bucks?" The postal employee was touched. He showed the letter to his fellow workers and they all kicked in a few dollars each, raised three hundred dollars, and sent it to the family. The boy wrote another letter to God, thanking Him for the recent infusion of cash, but ended with this request. "Next time, would you send the money directly to us? If you send it to the post office, they deduct two hundred dollars."

[Light-Work]

It's as hard for us to give as it is to open a space inside to let others give to us. So many times we want to give, but do we want to accept from someone else? Do you open yourself up to receive with no strings attached? Do you know how to say: "thank you?" Sometimes, we think that since we've been given a gift, the giver expects something in return. A person who doesn't want to receive stops the flow of Light just as quickly as someone who doesn't want to give. So keep it simple: find a place in yourself to give, and when someone gives to you, say: "thank you" and accept the gift with no strings attached.

For me, writing this book is an opportunity to share. It's a gift. There is something special about opening up and sharing with people. You, as the reader of the book and a participant in the *Living Kabbalah System*, have given me an opportunity to share Kabbalah with you—and in that way I've become the receiver.

Imagine that you were never allowed to give to a friend or share with anyone. How would you feel? And how would your friends feel if they were never allowed to give to you? Write in your journal what it would be like if you could not share with others, and how you predict those close to you would feel under the circumstances.

Create what we call a *giving log*. On one side, write down the ways in which you gave to others in the last 24 hours. On the other side, write down the ways in which you allowed others to give to you. Now you can see how much time you spent in unconditional sharing with others and how much you spent in unconditional receiving. A good long-term goal would be to make at least half of what we do in this world be directed toward assisting others.

We're all aspiring to be our best selves, the best versions we can be. That's what should be driving us constantly. We come to this world with the potential to be like the Creator. Our choices and actions either prevent us from reaching this end or propel us to become all that we were meant to be.

Chapter 23

Making this Last

As part of the last Light-Work, we created a giving log. What did you discover? Did you have a constant flow of sharing and receiving? That's one of the secrets of creating a continuous flow of Light in your life and in this world.

After much hard work, we've reached our final chapter. Whether you've gone through the program in this book in twenty-three days or a week or six months, this has been a very personal journey of discovery and insight. I hope it's been fun, uncomfortable, and revealing! It's important that we have a chance to acknowledge what you've accomplished and the courage, commitment, time, and effort it took to go through each of the Light-Work exercises. Look at your journal and see how filled every page is with thoughts, feelings, memories, experiences and insights. This is going to be a valuable tool for you.

A Review

In order to ensure that we don't forget everything that we've discussed, let's take a minute to review the territory we've covered.

We started off with the difference between short-term fulfillment and lasting fulfillment. We all seek instant gratification. Yet, if we're honest with ourselves, the short-term gratification that we so often rely on for happiness just doesn't do the trick. Giving up instant gratification takes discipline and effort, but the fulfillment we find as a result will stay with us. Sure, it's easy to get a rush of adrenaline, a quick fix. But we know, according to Kabbalah, that anything that we seek to get instantly is never going to last. It's a Universal Law.

The second stop on our journey was understanding the cosmic law of cause and effect. Nothing happens randomly or suddenly in this Universe. There are no accidents. Our purpose in life is to be to the cause of everything that we manifest; we don't want to become the effect. This means saying goodbye to being life's victim. It also means that we become the writers of our own movie script; we create our own reality. When we find ourselves starting to blame others, we've given up control of our lives.

Being a spiritual person means taking control and responsibility for everything in our life. No longer can we see life as something happening to us. But even when we recognize and understand that we're the cause, sometimes we get hoodwinked by the force that we refer to as the Opponent, the Ego. Throughout this book, we've gone to great lengths to dismantle our ego—we have even sought ways to embarrass ourselves to this end. We learned that sometimes we must do the most ridiculous, illogical things in order to break the control that our ego has over us. By crushing the ego, we connect to a world the kabbalists call the 99 percent.

The 99 Percent world is a metaphysical world of miracles, lasting joy, and happiness. This reality is one of two worlds that the kabbalists say exist in parallel dimensions. The other is the 1 Percent limited world of the five senses. As we learn to navigate through these parallel dimensions, we know that we'll experience certain tests and face many obstacles. Rather than being frustrated by these challenges, we recognize that this is part of our journey, and these are necessary stops along the way to our destination of ultimate fulfillment. We didn't make a wrong turn.

We learned that living in the 1 Percent world means living in a world of reaction. But we no longer want to live according to hasty, unthinking responses—where life is merely happening to us. Rather than be under the control of the ego, we want to be proactively engaged in life. We learned that proactive living connects us to the 99 Percent world of immense fulfillment.

We learned how to stop, as if we're watching ourselves on a TV screen, and click the pause button on the remote control. During this pause, we ask ourselves: *Is this the only way I can handle this situation? Is this how I want to be responding right now? We also remind ourselves: I have the capacity to be proactive in my life, to choose how I'm going to respond, to decide for myself which relationships are meaningful, and to decide who is in my life. If I don't want a particular person or circumstance in my life, then I need to be the one to change that.*

Challenging people and circumstances will always be a part of life. The people who push our buttons and upset us are all there by design. They represent opportunities for us to overcome our reactive, reflexive nature—chances to transform and overcome whatever it is we're here to correct. Only by having our buttons pushed can we know what it is that we're supposed to fix. Aggravating situations are alarm bells telling us it is time to elevate our consciousness by looking at the bigger picture. In this way we connect to the spiritual realm of that 99 Percent of the Light—the source of all our creativity, inspiration, openness, love, intuition, and joy.

We are vessels, based upon a built-in Desire to Receive divine goodness; but we also want to have a strong desire to share as much as we possibly can. Yes, it's natural for us to receive. That's what being a vessel is all about. But we also have the capacity to choose how much we receive and how much we share. We have the ability to create a constant state of circuitry, of continuity, much like a light bulb that maintains its glow.

Finally, we recognized what it means to truly share. It's not about how much we're doing and how much we're giving. We give of ourselves not because it's the right and moral thing to do, but because if we don't, we sacrifice our happiness. We become stuck. We become imprisoned in our comfort zone. True sharing is not based upon what we're going to get in return. It is selfless in nature.

Just like our desire to spread good news, when we tap into the 99 Percent realm, we want to share the fulfillment we found there. We want to do for others and share with others—and not because we'll look good in the process or because we'll be acknowledged for it.

We do it because the joyous energy that we have discovered is meant to be shared. And that's what will allow us to grow, expand, and be the best version of ourselves.

Living Kabbalah

Living Kabbalah has been about coming out of the darkness. Take a moment to look around and to see the shifts you have made in your life, your thoughts, and in your awareness.

Is Light really what you thought it was?

Early on in this book, we asked you to write down what you wanted to receive in life, what your desires were. Go back to your journal now and look at what you wrote. Is that still what you want? Has anything shifted in your understanding of desire or has your perspective changed? I'm sure you'll notice a difference. Oliver Wendell Holmes said that man's mind stretched to a new idea never goes back to its original dimensions. This book was designed to spiritually stretch you. Hopefully, you now know what it is that you are here to do, what your true purpose is, and the gifts that you are to share with the world.

We've come up with several different ways to help you hold onto what you've learned and ways to remember and embody these teachings:

- Remember what real fulfillment is, and be grateful for the abundance around you.

- Catch yourself in those robotic reactions to challenges and obstacles and use your k-Tools to find true, proactive solutions.
- Learn to love your garbage, to own it and embrace it in order to transform it into gifts. Look for the layers of filth and negativity that can accumulate.
- Don't fall into complacency. Remember, life is like a downward escalator. The minute that we take a rest, we go back down into our reactive nature.
- Remember gratitude and appreciation.
- Make sure your spiritual Desire to Receive is focused on giving and sharing.
- Make it last.

One of the ways that you can make it last is to go through this book again and repeat the Light-Work. I guarantee that each time you go through it, you will find things you didn't discover before.

Let me end with a story about the great kabbalist the Baal Shem Tov when he knew he was leaving this world. He handed different jobs to his students. "You'll be the ones giving the sermons. You'll be the ones teaching the people," he said as he divided up the tasks. To one of his students, he left the task of telling the stories of the Baal Shem Tov. The student asked the master: "How will I know my job is done?" The master smiled at him and said: "You'll know, you'll know."

So the student went all over the world spreading the stories of the Baal Shem Tov. He knew he hadn't finished his job because nothing significant happened. One day, he heard about a person who rewarded storytellers handsomely for stories about the Baal Shem Tov. The student arrived on a Friday. After dinner, his host said: "Tell me a story." But the student went blank. He realized the Opponent was blocking him from remembering. When he went to sleep that night, he cried: "What do I need to do to correct this?"

The next morning came and the two men ate breakfast. Once again he drew a blank when asked to tell a story. The same thing happened at lunch and at dinner. Sunday morning, they had brunch and still he couldn't remember a single story. So he got on his horse and started to leave town. Then he remembered something and galloped back.

He said to the man: "I remember something. The strange thing is, I don't remember the beginning and I don't remember the end, I just remember the middle," he began. "We were at a town that was about to be destroyed by an enemy's army. They were going to slaughter men, women, and children. The Baal Shem Tov sent one of his students to talk to the leader of the impending massacre, to tell him that the Baal Shem Tov was there and needed to speak to him. Sure enough, the leader of the army agreed to meet with the Baal Shem Tov. After meeting with him, the leader changed his mind: 'We're not going to touch this town,' he said.

The storyteller paused, "And that's all I remember of the story."

The man who heard the story started weeping. He said, "I was the leader of that massacre. I was going to kill the men, women, and children. When the Baal Shem Tov came to me, he said: 'There's still hope. If you stop now, change your ways, and start thinking of others, you can cleanse all of your negativity. You can turn all of your anger and negativity into gifts, which you can then share with the whole world."

Upon hearing this story from the former military leader, the student of the Baal Shem Tov knew his job was done. Like the man who stood before him, he had been transformed by the words of the great kabbalist.

Many of us try to do good but question if we're on the right path. "Are we really accomplishing anything? Is our work done? Should we keep going?" The truth is that the Universe will show us when we are done. We'll know by the immense joy that we feel inside.

[Light-Work]

Just when you thought your Light-Work exercises were over, I would like to propose a final exercise. Make a commitment to yourself to decide how you will continue your journey of spiritual growth and evolution. What are the next steps you will take? Who will you choose to support you in your journey? How will your life be different as a result of this commitment? When you connect to why you're committed to this work, it will help you to stay on your path. Finally, ask yourself in this Light-Work: With whom will I share this wisdom? We learn in Kabbalah that one of the secrets to holding on to this knowledge is to share it. The *Zohar* teaches us that one of the most powerful ways to reveal Light for ourselves is by teaching someone else how to overcome his or her own reactive nature and change their reality.

I thank you for allowing me to share this wisdom with you. I invite you to continue the spirit of sharing by visiting www.72.com to share your stories and experiences or to receive more information. Or pick up the phone and call 1-800-Kabbalah, our student support center, and say that Yehuda sent you.

One of the gifts that we've received from Kabbalah is recognizing that life does have a purpose. Hopefully, through this journey, you've discovered your unique mission and your beautiful gifts. Remember Michelangelo's gift to us: his sculpture of David, which he "discovered" beneath the excess rock. Take a moment now to see what you've uncovered in yourself. Do you see the Creator's divine potential? I do.

More from Best-Selling Author Yehuda Berg

The Prayer of the Kabbalist: The 42 - Letter Name of God

According to the ancient wisdom of Kabbalah, the powerful prayer known as *Ana Bekho'ah* invokes The 42-Letter Name of God, which connects to no less than the undiluted force of creation. By tapping into this connection through the Prayer, you can leave the past behind and make a fresh start. If you recite the Prayer on a regular basis, you are able to use the force of creation to create miracles, both in your everyday life and in the world at large. This book explains the meaning behind the 42 letters and gives you practical steps for how best to connect to their power.

The Power of Kabbalah

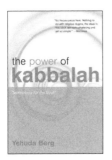

Imagine your life filled with unending joy, purpose, and contentment. Imagine your days infused with pure insight and energy. This is *The Power of Kabbalah*. It is the path from the momentary pleasure that most of us settle for, to the lasting fulfillment that is yours to claim. Your deepest desires are waiting to be realized. Find out how, in this basic introduction to the ancient wisdom of Kabbalah.

Kabbalah on Pain: How to Use It to Lose It

Learn how to use your emotional pain to your advantage and how to release its grip on you forever. When you avoid, ignore, or bury your pain, you only prolong psychic agony. But Kabbalah teaches a method for detaching from the source of this pain—human ego—and thereby forcing ego to take on and deal with your pain. When you choose the path of the soul where only ego suffers, you will begin to move toward the state of pure joy that is your destiny.

Kabbalah on Love

This charming little book has a simple yet profound message: Love is not something you learn or acquire but an essence within, waiting to be revealed. Buried by layers of ego, fear, shame, doubt, low self-esteem, and other limitations, the incredibly powerful force that is love can only be activated by sharing and serving unconditionally. Only then will the layers fall away and the essence of love reveal itself. The book draws the distinction between love and need, which is a selfish product of ego, and reminds us that we cannot love someone else until we figure out how to love ourselves and connect with the love within.

The Kabbalah Book of Sex: & Other Mysteries of the Universe

According to Kabbalah, the key to fulfilling sex lies in self awareness, not simply technique. Sex is the most powerful way to experience the Light of the Creator, and one of the most powerful ways to transform the world. *The Kabbalah Book of Sex* provides a solid foundation for understanding the origins of sex and its purpose, as well as practical kabbalistic tools to ignite your sex life. This ground-breaking guide teaches how to access higher levels of connection—to ourselves, our partners, and to spirit—and achieve unending passion, profound pleasure, and true fulfillment.

Rebooting: Defeating Depression with the Power of Kabbalah

An estimated 18 million people in the United States suffer from depression—that's almost 10% of the population. So chances are good that you have, or someone you know has, been affected by it. Antidepressants, counseling, herbal remedies—all have been known to help treat the symptoms, but sometimes they fall short. If only you could click on the "Restart" button and get your internal software back on track. Now, in *Rebooting*, noted kabbalistic scholar and author Yehuda Berg shows how you can do just that by reconnecting with desire and light to emerge from this debilitating darkness.

Angel Intelligence

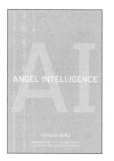

Discover how billions of angels exist and shape the world, and how, through your thoughts and deeds, you have the power to create them, whether positive or negative. You'll learn their individual names and characteristics and their unique roles, as well as how to call on them for different purposes and use them as powerful spiritual tools for transformation. By becoming aware of the angel dynamics at work in the universe and by learning how to connect with these unseen energy forces, you will gain amazing insight and the ability to meet life's greatest challenges.

The 72 Names of God: Technology for the Soul™

The 72 Names of God are not "names" in any ordinary sense, but a state-of-the-art technology that deeply touches the human soul and is the key to ridding yourself of depression, stress, stagnation, anger, and many other emotional and physical problems. The Names represent a connection to the infinite spiritual current that flows through the universe. When you correctly bring these power sources together, you are able to gain control over your life and transform it for the better.

The Living Kabbalah System™: Levels 1 & 2

Take Your Life to the Next Level™ with this step-by-step, 23-day system for transforming your life and achieving lasting fulfillment.

Created by Yehuda Berg and based on his belief that Kabbalah should be lived, not merely studied, this revolutionary interactive system incorporates the latest learning strategies, addressing all three learning styles:

- Auditory (recorded audio sessions)

- Visual (workbook with written concepts and graphics)

- Tactile (written exercises, self-assessments, and physical tools)

The sturdy carrying case makes the system easy and convenient to use, in the car, at the gym, on a plane, wherever and whenever you choose. Learn from today's great Kabbalah leaders in an intimate, one-on-one learning atmosphere. You get practical, actionable tools and exercises to integrate the wisdom of Kabbalah into your daily life. In just 23 days you can learn to live with greater intensity, be more successful in business and relationships, and achieve your dreams. Why wait? Take your life to the next level starting today.

More Books that can help you bring the wisdom of Kabbalah into your life

Immortality: The Inevitability of Eternal Life
By Rav Berg

This book will totally change the way in which you perceive the world, if you simply approach its contents with an open mind and an open heart.

Most people have it backwards, dreading and battling what they see as the inevitability of aging and death. But, according to the great Kabbalist Rav Berg and the ancient wisdom of Kabbalah, it is eternal life that is inevitable.

With a radical shift in our cosmic awareness and the transformation of the collective consciousness that will follow, we can bring about the demise of the death force once and for all—in this "lifetime."

God Wears Lipstick: Kabbalah for Women
By Karen Berg

For thousands of years, women were banned from studying Kabbalah, the ancient source of wisdom that explains who we are and what our purpose is in this universe. Karen Berg changed that. She opened the doors of The Kabbalah Centre to all who would seek to learn.

In *God Wears Lipstick*, Karen Berg shares the wisdom of Kabbalah, especially as it affects you and your relationships. She reveals a woman's special place in the universe and why women have a spiritual advantage over men. She explains how to find your soulmate and your purpose in life, and empowers you to become a better human being.

The Secret: Unlocking the Source of Joy & Fulfillment
By Michael Berg

The Secret reveals the essence of life in its most concise and powerful form. Several years before the latest "Secret" phenomenon, Michael Berg shared the amazing truths of the world's oldest spiritual wisdom in this book. In it, he has pieced together an ancient puzzle to show that our common understanding of life's purpose is actually backwards, and that anything less than complete joy and fulfillment can be changed by correcting this misperception.

Secrets of the Zohar: Stories and Meditations to Awaken the Heart
By Michael Berg

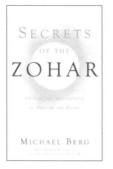

The Zohar's secrets are the secrets of the Bible, passed on as oral tradition and then recorded as a sacred text that remained hidden for thousands of years. They have never been revealed quite as they are here in these pages, which decipher the codes behind the best stories of the ancient sages and offer a special meditation for each one. Entire portions of the *Zohar* are presented, with the Aramaic and its English translation in side-by-side columns. This allows you to scan and to read aloud so that you can draw on the *Zohar*'s full energy and achieve spiritual transformation. Open this book and open your heart to the Light of the *Zohar*!

Wheels of a Soul
By Rav Berg

In *Wheels of a Soul*, Kabbalist Rav Berg explains why we must acknowledge and explore the lives we have already lived in order to understand the life we are living today. Make no mistake: You have been here before. Just as science is now beginning to recognize that time and space may be nothing but illusions, Rav Berg shows why death itself is the greatest illusion of all.

The Zohar

Composed more than 2,000 years ago, the *Zohar* is a set of 23 books, a commentary on biblical and spiritual matters in the form of conversations among spiritual masters. But to describe the *Zohar* only in physical terms is greatly misleading. In truth, the *Zohar* is nothing less than a powerful tool for achieving the most important purposes of our lives. It was given to all humankind by the Creator to bring us protection, to connect us with the Creator's Light, and ultimately to fulfill our birthright of true spiritual transformation.

More than eighty years ago, when The Kabbalah Centre was founded, the *Zohar* had virtually disappeared from the world. Few people in the general population had ever heard of it. Whoever sought to read it—in any country, in any language, at any price—faced a long and futile search.

Today all this has changed. Through the work of The Kabbalah Centre and the editorial efforts of Michael Berg, the *Zohar* is now being brought to the world, not only in the original Aramaic language but also in English. The new English *Zohar* provides everything for connecting to this sacred text on all levels: the original Aramaic text for scanning; an English translation; and clear, concise commentary for study and learning.

The Kabbalah Centre

The International Leader in the Education of Kabbalah

Since its founding, The Kabbalah Centre has had a single mission: to improve and transform people's lives by bringing the power and wisdom of Kabbalah to all who wish to partake of it.

Through the lifelong efforts of Kabbalists Rav and Karen Berg, and the great spiritual lineage of which they are a part, an astonishing 3.5 million people around the world have already been touched by the powerful teachings of Kabbalah. And each year, the numbers are growing!

• • • •

If you were inspired by this book in any way and would like to know how you can continue to enrich your life through the wisdom of Kabbalah, here is what you can do next:

Call 1-800-KABBALAH where trained instructors are available 18 hours a day. These dedicated people are willing to answer any and all questions about Kabbalah and help guide you along in your effort to learn more.

NOTES:

NOTES:

NOTES:

_____

_____

_____

_____

_____

_____

_____

_____

_____

_____

_____

_____

_____

_____

_____

_____

_____

_____

_____

_____

_____

NOTES:

NOTES:

NOTES:

NOTES:

In memory of my parents, Pablo and Susana,
may their souls be elevated by the Light
that is revealed from the wisdom in this book—and
the spiritual work and transformation that it inspires.